THOR RAMSEY'S

TOTAL
MONEY
MELTDOWN

D1384246

THOR RAMSEY'S
TOTAL MONEY MELTDOWN

A PROVEN PLAN FOR FINANCIAL DISASTER
(AND RECOVERY)

THOR RAMSEY

MOODY PUBLISHERS

CHICAGO

All Scripture quotations, unless otherwise indicated, are taken from the *Holy Bible, New International Version*®. NIV®. Copyright ©1973, 1978, 1984 by Biblica, Inc.™ Used by permission of Zondervan. All rights reserved worldwide.

Scripture quotations marked ESV are taken from *The Holy Bible, English Standard Version*. Copyright © 2000, 2001 by Crossway Bibles, a division of Good News Publishers. Used by permission. All rights reserved.

Scripture quotations marked NKJV are taken from the *New King James Version*. Copyright © 1982 by Thomas Nelson, Inc. Used by permission. All rights reserved.

Library of Congress Cataloging-in-Publication Data
Ramsey, Thor.
  Thor Ramsey's total money meltdown : a proven plan for financial disaster (and recovery) /
  Thor Ramsey.
    p. cm.
  Summary: "If Christian comedian Thor Ramsey could recommend only one book on escaping debt and surviving a financial meltdown, he'd recommend Dave Ramsey's Total Money Makeover. But for readers who want a more humorous look at retaking control of the household budget, well, he humbly recommends his own Total Money Meltdown. After all, he won't be able to repay his debts from the sales of Dave Ramsey's book. Thor Ramsey's sidesplitting guide to financial recovery chronicles his own bad financial decisions and what it took him to climb out of the hole he dug. ('By the way, you should only dig holes if you plan on filling them with treasure.') Not just a vehicle for his wit and humor, Thor Ramsey's Total Money Meltdown also provides readers with the necessary tools and biblical motivation to become financially free. The truth is that all of us who've been in financial trouble knew better. But sometimes we don't know what it takes to get out of the hole. We feel hopeless and overwhelmed. This book shines some funny hope into people's messy money lives, first as a 'how not-to guide' and then as a 'how-to recover guide.' "—Provided by publisher.
  Includes bibliographical references.
  ISBN 978-0-8024-0075-8 (pbk.)
  1. Finance, Personal--Humor. I. Title. II. Title: Total money meltdown.
  HG179.R3158 2011
  32.024—dc22

                                              2011004286

Also available as an EBook 978-0-8024-8111-5

Edited by Pam Pugh
Cover and Interior Design: Smartt Guys design

We hope you enjoy this book from Moody Publishers. Our goal is to provide high-quality, thought-provoking books and products that connect truth to your real needs and challenges. For more information on other books and products written and produced from a biblical perspective, go to www.moodypublishers.com or write to:

Moody Publishers
820 N. LaSalle Boulevard
Chicago, IL 60610

1 3 5 7 9 10 8 6 4 2

Printed in the United States of America

For my lovely girls, Eden Olivia and Kate Tulip.

I hope this book puts you both through college.

CONTENTS

PART THREE: **MONEY AND YOUR DREAMS**
(or You Can't Afford Dreams, So Get Back to Work)

PART FOUR: **MONEY AND YOUR HABITS**
(or Do What Your Money Says: Trust God)

"ARE YOU RELATED TO DAVE RAMSEY?"

(Then I Show Them My Checkbook and They Laugh)

....

During the housing boom, my wife, Dinika, and I flipped four homes. We were debt free. We had money in the bank. We were ahead of the game. Then we renovated our kitchen.

Wow.

We have a nice kitchen.

No food.

But a great place to think about food.

We made some really, really, really bad decisions, which I discovered one day when I noticed we didn't have any money left.

Our financial crisis was real. The economy took a nosedive (often referred to as a downturn, a less ominous word than *nosedive*), and work was less frequent than in boom time. I'm not so sure the job I have now is even considered work by many people. Most job conversations I have go like this: "Whatta ya do for a living?"

"I'm a stand-up comedian."

"Oh, that must be fun. How do you support your family?"

My mother. She still doesn't get it. Cue snare drum.

The agency that booked my comedy shows imploded, owing me three months' worth of pay. We had no savings. We were in the hole with credit card debt. Our cash flow was *kaput*, which is a German word for "it's in the kitchen." Instead of going with another agency, I decided to start booking my own shows. Soon, I realized how my dependency had been on the "agency" and not on God.

Did I really believe that God was our provider? I certainly believed the Lord sent us trouble when we needed it for the sake of our spiritual lives. The question I had now was, "Would He send a check?" One thing was certain: Our financial struggle took the idea of praying for daily bread from belief to experience. The fear became "What does daily bread mean to God?" You can get daily bread if you have a list of homeless shelters. My lack of trust made me think, *Maybe we don't have a money problem. Maybe we have a heart problem.*

As a married couple, we each played our part when it came to money. Dinika handled the money and I ignored it. That's the nitty-gritty of a money meltdown. I neglected to stay abreast of our financial situation until there was a problem. I never even looked at our online account, because, quite simply, it felt like homework.

One day we looked at each other and asked, "How do we get out of this mess? If this keeps up, Capital One is going to keep us in for recess."

Naturally, in our search we turned to the experts.

I bought one of Suze Orman's books, *The 9 Steps to Financial Freedom.* There was another book I should have read first called *The 2 Steps to Getting through a Book with 9 Steps.* Her book was somewhat helpful. Even though I never got past page 30, I did manage to balance our checkbook. So we're good for another three years.

Through the hand of Providence, I happened to have two complimentary copies of Dave Ramsey's book *Total Money Makeover.* My wife and I decided to read them instead of fight.

It was a good decision.

But the "hand of Providence"? C'mon, Thor. Really?

Here's what happened (with only minor embellishments):

Three years ago, comedian Taylor Mason and I were touring thirty cities together. Backstage at one of the shows, hundreds of copies of Dave Ramsey's *Total Money Makeover* were piled everywhere. We couldn't sit down without sitting on a stack of Dave's books. Who says God isn't obvious? There Taylor and I sat backstage discussing the things comedians discuss, like the tour, if it was worth continuing or not—some shows are well-attended, others not so much—money, debate, future of tour, how it takes time to build an audience, and so on.

There we were, sitting on a stack of books about financial planning and discussing money. The pastor, a wiser man than either of us, gave us each a copy of Dave's book.

It's like the old joke about the guy who is stranded on an island and prays for God to rescue him. Then a ship comes along and offers to bring him aboard, but the man says, "No, thank you. I'm trusting that God will rescue me." Then a plane lands, one of those water-landing planes, and offers to give him a lift, but the man says, "No, thank you. I'm trusting that God will rescue me." Then a sub, really asking for directions, offers him a ride. Again, he declines by saying, "No, thank you. I'm trusting that God will rescue me." Finally, the man discovers a local tribe on the other side of the island, marries one of its inhabitants, a pretty young woman named Konocte, has ten kids, grows old, and dies.

When he gets to heaven, the man asks God, "Why didn't You rescue me?" God says, "Are you kidding? Do you really think that your bad decisions can hinder My will? Didn't you believe that all things work for the good to those who love Me and are called according to My purposes? That whole shipwreck thing didn't catch Me off guard. I know how thick-headed you are, that you'd reject every way off the island that came around. Sometimes My help is so obvious you fail to see it. Yet that doesn't prevent Me from helping you. If the stupidity and sin of mankind could prevent Me from doing anything, I wouldn't be much of a God, now would I? Besides, you wouldn't have met Konocte had you left the island, now would you? Wasn't she worth the price of living in a remote tropical paradise? Trust Me, you wouldn't have been any happier back in Minot."

Or it goes something like that anyway.

We began talking together about money, making financial decisions together, climbing out of debt together . . . but not without the help of God.

So I took the book home and never read it. I placed it on my bookshelf with every intention of forgetting about it.

About a year later I was at a conference where Dave Ramsey spoke, and he gave the entire audience a copy of this same book. Never one to turn down a free book, I took it home and placed it on my bookshelf next to the last free copy I'd received. If I could forget about it once, I was sure I could forget about it twice.

Then it happened.

I was at my desk manning the phone, staring at things in my office when I noticed the two copies of Dave's book. They were still sitting there on my bookshelf. I was reminded, "Hey, we're in a financial crisis." It seemed like an ideal time to read them. One for my wife and one for me. Let's see who finishes first. Winner take all.

Oh, that's right. We got no money.

Well, we read it anyway.

Dave's book helped us slowly face the reality of our situation, the blood and guts of living from paycheck to paycheck with an irregular income, which makes things even more exciting. We began talking together about money, making financial decisions together, climbing out of debt together . . . but not without the help of God. "Thou shalt not murder" should always be highlighted in anyone's Bible during a financial crisis.

Or maybe that's just us.

Now, some of you may be asking, "Why Dave Ramsey? Why not some other financial guru?"

For me, Dave Ramsey was the first financial guru I read who didn't make me roll my eyes. So many financial gurus take this attitude that "you deserve the best in life, so just get your finances in harmony with the moon's seventh alignment of your inner wolf's outer ring." Or something like that. Dave told me in a very direct but kind way that being broke was my fault. But that if we took the steps, sacrificed, followed the truth about finances, then we could create new financial habits.

Dinika and I took inventory and discovered some of our financial fallacies, such as believing a budget means once we are out of money we can't buy anything else until we get some more money. That was our budget. Spend as much as you make.

Then there were the year-end tax receipts that revealed our spiritual attitudes. We hadn't tithed 10 percent. It was just above 5 percent. It felt like 10, but the receipts tell no lies. One statistic I heard said that the average American evangelical tithes about 2 percent to their local church. That says a lot about ushers. Pass the plate, calculate, and if it's short, then pass it back. Do your job, guys! It also says a lot about the heart of the American church. "Is it even mandatory to tithe 10 percent? Aren't we under grace now?"

Maybe you're in the same situation. If so, it's time to take some drastic steps.

Dave didn't tell us anything we didn't already know, which made us feel less dumb for losing all our money. We knew what to do. We just didn't do it. Dave reminded us of that. Then we felt dumb for losing all our money.

Still, it must be asked, "If we knew what to do, then why didn't we do it?" That's the question that reveals the spiritual nature of money. If you want to know where your heart's at, look at your checkbook. Apparently, my heart was in overdraft protection. Follow the trail of your money, and you'll find your heart's true desire, which is a nice way of saying, "Idol." If we spend most of our money on personal amusements, behold your idol. I only bought that golden calf to put my feet up on while I watch our new 52-inch flat screen high-definition television. I don't worship it. It doesn't even have a place for drinks.

Maybe you're in the same situation.

If so, it's time to take some drastic steps.

Here's the first step in my plan for recovery from a total money melt-down: Buy another one of my books to give to a friend. I'm sure you know someone upside-down on their home loan. It's only half the country. This will be a great encouragement to them.

Good. Now that that's out of the way, ask yourself this one simple question: "Do I know anybody else who might need a copy of this book? Anyone? Just one more person?"

Even though the light at the end of the tunnel was blocked by bills, and bankruptcy peeked around the corner, my wife and I began our journey toward debt-free living. Many days, but only if you count them all, we felt like giving up. We were doing it together, but we felt alone.

That's when I decided to start writing about it. I wanted a detailed story of people like us, a couple who followed Dave's plan and made hard decisions based on it, like skipping Starbucks once. How did they find the courage to do it? What did they drink that day? Didn't they get a headache in the afternoon?

I started keeping a journal of our progress and setbacks. Most people feel alone when they're digging themselves out of debt. To help people feel less alone, I decided to share the shame of our financial ruin with the world. My wife wasn't so crazy about the idea, but then I told her that a publisher would give us an advance for sharing our shame. And she still hated the idea.

Then I reminded her what the famous screenwriter and director Elia Kazan once said: "The writer, when he is an artist, is someone who admits what others don't dare reveal."

"Just don't let my mother see it," she said.

So, to amend Kazan: "The writer, when he is an artist, is someone who admits what others don't dare reveal—but not to his mother-in-law. No writer needs to be that stupid."

It's not an easy journey.

The first few chapters of Dave's book made me feel intense regret. (So, I'd skip those if I were you.) There was no reason for us to be in this situation. Twice in the last five years we were completely debt free. We could be so far ahead. It just beats you down when you think about it. So you buy an issue of *Guns & Ammo* and fantasize about owning a firearm on the day they come to evict you from your home. Well, you go to the library anyway. Who has money for magazines these days?

Right now losing our home is only a daydream, but sometimes I wake up at five a.m. and can't go back to sleep because of this daydream. So, *daydream* doesn't seem quite the right word. And nightmares happen while you're asleep. Is there such a thing as daymares? So I don't know what you call these thoughts. Rational fears? That seems too . . . rational.

Sin.

Is anxiety sin?

From what I can tell, "be anxious for nothing" is a command.

After reading the next chapters of Dave's book, I began to feel hope, a long hope delayed until sometime in the future, but hope nonetheless. A hope without firearms involved. Because my wife and I read the book together, we were finally able to discuss money.

We were on the same page.

I'm not sure what you call a book like this one where you learn from the tragedy of others. A comedy show? A "how-not-to" book? Maybe you've felt like the only other financial dupe on the planet. Take heart; you've found your leader. Few can top my idiocy. I can give good financial advice because I've had lots of experience losing money. This is most definitively a "how-not-to" book.

This book is also a field guide to financial repentance (with jokes). It's a before-and-after photo of a former financial bulimic who would binge on goods and services and then empty his bank account. The weight of my checkbook would fluctuate. But then I learned how to eat my money . . . okay, this analogy is breaking down. The point is, we recovered financially.

Thor Ramsey's Total Money Meltdown chronicles our bad financial decisions and our climb out of the hole we dug. My editor asked me, "Are you sure you want to reveal all this?" But what, ultimately, is going to remain hidden? From a biblical standpoint, everything will one day come to light, even if you don't pay the electric bill. There's no use hiding if "everything is uncovered and laid bare before the eyes of him to whom we must give account,"[1] and that includes financial statements.

The truth is, we all know better. But sometimes we don't know what it takes to get out of the mess. We feel hopeless and overwhelmed. I hope this book shines some funny hope into people's messy money lives by using my own life, first as a "how-not-to" guide, and then as a "how-to-recover" guide.

People want to know that other people are as dumb as they are—and I am. But it isn't just a problem of bad financial decisions. It is a spiritual issue, "for where your treasure is, there your heart will be also,"[2] which I've found to be the key to all financial issues.

I'm sure there's a spiritual reason to go to Starbucks daily.

I just haven't found it.

Yet.

In a sense, my editor is right. This is messy and embarrassing stuff. It's not easy climbing out of debt, creating new money habits, and turning your finances around. Our marriage suffered duress. Days and nights were filled with anxiety. Yet, in the midst of it all, I never gave up Starbucks. This alone showed my resolve to overcome the odds.

Don't you love happy endings?

PART ONE:

ANATOMY OF A MONEY MELTDOWN

(or Build Your Self-Esteem by Reading about My Financial Life)

1

HOW DID WE GET HERE?
(And Why Didn't My Wallet Come Along?)

....

You know you've experienced a total money meltdown when you're no longer welcome at Starbucks. That's how a total money meltdown works. I walked into Starbucks, got in line, and waved hello to the familiar faces in kelly green aprons. They know me, so when I get to the barista, she hands me my daily venti iced chai tea. I hand her my debit card and take a big sip of my chai tea while waiting for my card to clear, which it doesn't.

So there I am with a mouth full of iced chai tea that's not even mine.

How do you handle that situation? Do you spit it back into the cup? Do you swallow and pay for what you drank? Here's a good rule of thumb: Don't sip your drink until it's paid for. This way when they tell you your card's been declined you can avoid the spit-take. You don't want to be staring at your friendly neighborhood Starbucks barista, chai tea dripping down your face and no cash in your wallet.

Thus began my money meltdown awakening.

Now, you may be asking, "How did you end up in this situation?" People ask questions like this because they want to know how they, too, can accomplish the same goals.

So how did I get here?

The same way you can.

Follow this one simple step: DENIAL.

Denial is the thing that keeps us from facing our financial troubles. It's the only step you need to take if financial ruin is your goal. I know it sounds too good to be true, but it is. Denial is all you need to create money problems. That and a bunch of bills. You have to have something to deny.

Take it from me, living in denial is a lousy way to live.

Admit it; you don't want anyone to know that you're having financial problems. And why should you? It's none of their business. Wait a second. This isn't about me. Anyway, you don't have to go blabbing all your problems to everyone, but if you're married, you do have to go to your husband or wife and admit that you have been denying/ignoring/sticking your head in the sand/turning up the 50-inch HDTV that you just bought . . . doing everything but facing your financial problems. Then after you say this, don't say, "And you're that problem."

Take it from me, living in denial is a lousy way to live. Eventually, the tension of your checkbook catches up with you. Some people refer to this tension as reality, but let's not mince words. This is about reality versus denial. Until you face the reality of your financial situation, you will continue reasoning like this: A bill will come and you'll figure, "I can make it up next month." The second month comes and you say, "I can make it up next month." That third month comes and you say, "Well, I ruined my credit now, so . . . why even pay for the junk?"

Reality versus denial.

Seventy percent of Americans live from paycheck to paycheck, but somehow feel okay about how they're handling money. It's called denial. You may feel tired of living from paycheck to paycheck. Wait a second. You get a paycheck? That's amazing! You're already ahead of the game. And calling my family's financial security "a game" shows you how I got into this mess.

Denial keeps us from asking practical financial questions because we don't want to face the answers. Questions like, "If I lost my job tomorrow, how many months could I keep up with bills?"

If I lost my job tomorrow, I'd be a squatter.

Or questions like, "If my car or my roof failed today, what would I do?"

Walk. And get a pot. Next question?

In denial you will find your credit card denied. Apple computers denied my credit card in less than 30 seconds, even faster than Starbucks. I'm typing this on my 2004 PowerBook with the cracked-screen goop that gels around my desktop on the inside. I only have ¾ of a screen to work on. That's the reality of it. "How will you write a book on a laptop with only ¾ of a screen?" Shorter sentences.

Most of us have experienced the embarrassing situation of credit card denial. And if you haven't, I guess you're reading this just to feel better about yourself.

Congratulations. You're not me.

Usually, it goes down like this:

As the cashier at Target is scanning your items, you make small talk.

"How about that?"

"You ain't kiddin'."

Things along those lines.

Then: "Your card has been declined."

REJECTION

The established financial world has rejected you, but they are still thankful for your business. They want you in debt. Forever. Your self-esteem plummets, because in real life your self-esteem is tied to the Dow Jones Industrial Average, which is how your credit card company (also called a "bank") has arranged things, because this way you will strive to be accepted by them again someday. You are not a true American without plastic money. Target has called your patriotism into question. If you have a Target Visa, your face turns as red as the card. You blend in with the Target logo painted on the wall and slink out of the store, a headless shopper.

The good thing about credit card denial is that sometimes it snaps us out of DENIAL and gives us a total money meltdown awakening.

When you accept the reality that you're in a financial crisis, you will want to hide it from everyone, like we do when people invite us out to lunch after church and I have to say, "Sorry, it's not in the budget."

As if we even have a budget.

Facing reality helps. Putting up a front never does. Besides, your "best face forward" façade will always be found out. You can fool some of the people some of the time, but never the waitress at Applebee's.

"Your card was declined, sir."

"Well, that's a shame, because your food was eaten."

> **The most important thing I learned from this whole fiasco is that our hearts, not our bank accounts, determine our financial well-being.**

Me, I should have snapped out of denial sooner. I'd known for the last three years that if we didn't change things, we'd end up living an insecure, paycheck-to-paycheck, hope-we-can-keep-our-home existence, which we did. What good's a home if it's filled with insecurity, anger, resentment, and bitterness?

If you recognize yourself in any of the above scenarios or find yourself in a situation like ours, then be encouraged that there are other people in the world who use powdered milk. Welcome to the club. Here's the secret membership password: stop denying.

The most important thing I learned from this whole fiasco is that our hearts, not our bank accounts, determine our financial well-being. That's one reason it's so hard to examine our finances—they tell us so much about our hearts. Dinika and I were in a mess because of deeply ingrained attitudes and assumptions, like thinking my dad would write me a check to bail us out. He's been dead since I was eleven, so you can see how deeply ingrained these attitudes were. But we cannot improve our situation if we don't look at what our heart is financing.

If you want to take it further than behavior modification, then this book is really about the gospel and how our money managing either testifies that we get the gospel or we don't. And by "get" it I mean understand and embrace and submit to Christ as God in the flesh, who died on the cross in our place (justification), satisfied the wrath of God by doing so (propitiation), and rose again three days later that we might live new lives because God has given us new hearts (regeneration). You know? Get it. If we get it, our money managing habits will change. By repentance or the discipline of God's hand.

I'd suggest repentance, being a recipient of the latter.

Once you have a money meltdown awakening and snap out of denial, the first thing you will want to do is get out of debt fast. It's going to be discouraging at times. It will be humiliating. You have to have a rock-solid determination. You have to say to yourself, "I'll do anything that doesn't violate God's will to get out of debt!" Say that to yourself now. Out loud. "I'll do anything it takes to get out of debt."

What exactly will you have to do?

How humiliating is it going to get?

I can tell you this much. It all starts with the Census Bureau.

2

KEEPING YOUR PART-TIME JOB A SECRET
(So It Won't Ruin Your Career)

....

My wife and I haven't been good financial planners. Our initial plan was to homeschool our kids and charge 'em tuition. Apparently, there's some sort of state regulation against this. But we still home school. The financial upside is obvious. This way, when their lunch money is stolen . . . it stays in the family.

This book was my second plan. My plan was to write a humor book about getting out of debt and then use the advance from the publisher to get out of debt. After just a few pages into it, this plan didn't seem like a sound one either, since I haven't finished the book yet. This is all I have so far. Unless they want to publish a really short book:

My wife and I spent all our money, then this nice publisher gave us an advance, and now we're good. You should write a book. Thanks for reading. Hope that helped.

I wanted to get out of debt. There had to be some way that we can earn extra cash. Remember, if you want to get out of debt, you are going to have to look for creative ways to generate more income to pay down your debt.

I think my wife can get by with one kidney. That's right. Harvesting organs and selling them on the black market can supply our family with a second income. That's a creative idea.

Lemme ask my wife. I'll be right back.

Okay, that wasn't well received.

"Why not your kidney?" she said to me.

So at least she's open to the idea of selling a kidney. I just think it's a better sell to say, "This kidney belonged to a drop-dead gorgeous blonde."

Or I could get a job at Starbucks. But then I'd have to work forty hours a week and bring home maybe $300. That's no good. Besides, if I was at Starbucks right now blending your frappuccino, I wouldn't have time to write about not working there. Maybe there is another way.

What about selling our home?

We might be able to sell our home and make a profit, but I don't want to consider that yet. I like our home. We bought an old Victorian from 1898 and restored it. Victorians hold their market value better than subdivision homes because they're a specialty item. Of all the homes we've ever lived in, we love this one the most. Selling it is not something I want to think about right now.

"What about a second job?" asked my wife.

"Who'll watch the kids?"

"I meant for you."

A second job?

If you're a husband reading this and you take the idea that one of your roles in marriage is to provide for your family, you might begin asking God questions like I did. "Lord, I could quit being a comedian and do something else, but what else? What am I qualified to do?" I don't know what I'd do if I didn't do stand-up comedy. It's too late to turn back now.

What kind of job am I gonna get? I didn't listen to anybody when I was young, so I don't have a "fallback-on" plan. I have an idea of what kind of career I'd end up with, and that's the scary thing. "Hey, does anybody feel like pizza? I've got some pull with Domino's now."

What could I do and make the same amount of money? If I just quit without a plan, would that be presumptuous? "Please, Lord, make my path straight. And balance my checkbook." Okay, that last line wasn't part of the prayer, but you get the idea.

First I took the written test, which was filled with story problems that made me feel even more depressed, because, well, they were story problems.

There is this phrase Dave Ramsey repeats in his book several times: Live like no one else, so you can live like no one else. The idea behind it is that you make sacrifices now (which most of us don't, so when you do, you're living like no one else) so that later you won't be anchored down by debt (like most of us are, so when you're not, you're living like no one else). One of the sacrifices I decided to make to help pay off our debt faster was to apply for a temporary position with the US Census Bureau.

Uncle Sam wanted me.

I think that phrase was a compliment at one time.

That's right. To avoid financial ruin I became a government worker, which is kind of like taking a vow of silence to improve your marriage.

First I took the written test, which was filled with story problems that made me feel even more depressed, because, well, they were story problems. I was so depressed that I was relieved when they hired me.

So I walked into the first day of training at the US Census Bureau, which was basically a room of other depressed and hopeless people (mostly real estate agents) filling out paperwork. Honestly, I almost left and never came back. Why? Because it felt completely humiliating. I'm certainly not famous, but I hosted three seasons of a family comedy television series, so once in a while strangers will approach me and ask me if I'm Thor Ramsey, which I am.

But I wouldn't have been that day at the Census Bureau.

"Are you Thor Ramsey?"

"I do not know the man."

"You're not a comedian?"

I would have denied myself three times.

All the fears of what people will think came screaming into my mind: *If word gets out that I've taken a part-time job, people will think my comedy career is sputtering, about to take a nosedive. I'll be perceived as being dead in the water. Getting out of debt could hurt my career.*

That's just a sample of what ran through my head. The only comforting thought I had was, *Well, at least I'm not a real estate agent.*

Then I thought of my family, my responsibility to provide, to get us out of debt. I'll have nothing to provide my kids with if we don't get out of debt, that's for sure. So, I stayed, raised my right hand, and was sworn in as an official government employee, taking the same oath of office as representatives of Congress.

When I arrived home with an armful of papers the Census Bureau gave me, Dinika asked, "What's all that?"

I said, "I can't tell you because I work for the government now."

"Should I expect a scandal?"

"Well, I did take the same oath as a congressman."

Sworn to an oath of secrecy, because this census stuff is very touchy stuff. Do you want a group of strangers knowing how many people live in your home and what race they are?

It was my part-time job to count people of all races, red and yellow, black and white. And the Census Bureau has oodles of choices for race. *Please choose one.*

The census doesn't monitor religious affiliation. However, here's something interesting I learned during the training classes: As a census worker, I can't dispute what you say. If I ask some guy what race he is, and he says, "Cow," then I can't argue with him about it. I just mark the box and move on to the next question about how many extraterrestrials are living in his home.

The training itself was at points incredibly boring in a way that only the government can make something incredibly boring. The government seems to have standards of boring. Every document must be approved by the Committee for Boring Language Choices before it can become an official US training manual.

I believe that's how many of us get into these situations to begin with—we're concerned about what other people think.

The first day was the most humiliating.

"This is what my life has come to—government worker? Wait. That's not true. Part-time government worker."

Then my mind calmed down a bit. I'm told the location I'll be working from is another city, not the city I live in. This eliminates the fear of knocking on the door of someone I know.

"Hey, how's that comedy thing going?"

"Quiet, Cow Man."

Then the fear of being recognized surfaces again.

One weekend out of town, doing my main gig (I'm still a full-time comedian), my ride to the event picked me up at the airport and during the drive said, "I looked you up on the Web. I didn't realize you were famous."

"Well," I said, "if someone doesn't realize you're famous, then you're not famous. But thank you."

The thing I find comforting about Los Angeles is that it's full of famous people I've never heard of. *Dancing with the Stars*? I've never even heard of half of them, but they're stars. Fame is a very relative thing.

This lady who sat in front of me at the census training kept saying, "You look really familiar."

She said it three days in a row.

I just gave her a matter-of-fact "Hmmm."

But I think the humiliation of taking on another job is common among us humans. Who knows? Many of the people in the training class probably felt the same way I do.

They might have all been saying to themselves, *I hope no one recognizes him.*

I believe that's how many of us get into these situations to begin with—we're concerned about what other people think. That's why we have a good job (or did) and a nice home and two cars and 2.8 well-groomed children. (That third kid doesn't bathe as often.)

But we must face the reality of our own façade.

The truth is, this job helped pay down my pride more than anything.

TAKING
RESPONSIBILITY
(Then Misplacing It)

....

I n a money meltdown, you will want to blame someone. In this case, my wife is used to it. If I'm missing socks or can't find a hammer, or if the DVR failed to record the game, somehow these things are always her fault. But I can't blame Dinika, because, well, I married her. She can't blame me, because, well, it's not my fault. C'mon now! She handled the checkbook, which worked out great . . . for the economy.

Blaming someone else is misplacing your responsibility. Personally, I can't misplace my responsibility, because I've never taken any.

Along with climbing out of this financial hole, we are trying to stay married, which we've found much easier to do since we're broke. We can't afford a divorce. Blessing in disguise. Our marriage isn't in jeopardy, just our checkbook. I would never leave my wife for the simple reason that if I left her, then who would I blame for our financial crisis? Besides the government and Wall Street and the Federal Reserve? Still, it's only hypocritical to blame the government for something we're unwilling to do ourselves, like look for my socks. Also, handle money responsibly. Not to say that the government played no part in our financial crisis, both personally and nationally. But I'll get to that later. (Oh, my blame knows no bounds.)

The bottom line is that my wife and I are broke. We did not plan well. We spent all our money on Starbucks, I guess. That's who I can blame! Starbucks! Man, that coffee's good. Here's all our money! That might sound stupid to you, but what have you got to show for your money?

At least I'm awake.

As it turns out, being broke also keeps you up at night.

Who knew?

The second step (after facing your denial of the problem) is taking full responsibility. This situation is not your wife's fault. It's *my* wife's fault. I don't even know your wife. Wait a second. There I go again. Your greatest temptation in a total money meltdown is to blame someone, anyone, other than yourself. Take responsibility. This is your fault, Thor. That's why it's *Thor Ramsey's Total Money Meltdown*.

Ultimately, a man is responsible for his family, and that is where the blame should be laid—at the feet of a society that denies this truth. That's right. It's society's fault, not . . . there I go again. It's me. A man is responsible for his family, both materially and spiritually. As a baby-boomer male I hated this fact (as did my baby-boomer wife), but that is part of a deeper societal problem—men not taking responsibility for their families and women denying men responsibility. He had a mommy once, sweetheart, and you're not her.

When Dinika and I were dating, she had a great-paying job, a new car, a Jet Ski, and the image of being good with money. We always assume people with lots of toys are good with money. How else could they afford all those toys? I was just thankful that I found a woman who would keep my finances in line. You know, take care of me.

My father died when I was eleven, and being raised by a single mother subconsciously taught me a lesson that many boys learn: Women take care of you. Not just tenderly, the way they baby you when you're sick, but in every way, both financially and emotionally. This is probably why my wife gets blamed for my missing socks. So like many boys (not all) raised by single mothers, I grew up to be an irresponsible young man who dated women who took care of me. Sometimes I had to date more than one at a time so they could get the job done. I was a handful.

Now, this isn't to disparage single mothers who are doing the best they can as mothers while trying to fulfill the role of the absent men in their lives, too. My mother did the best she could under trying circumstances. Still, when men are absent through death or abandonment, or even when they are present but don't fulfill their God-given roles, the societal repercussions are whopping.

When my wife married me, I was a man who didn't talk about money and felt okay with a woman supporting me. I thought I was progressive.

For the longest time, I had difficulty relating to men. I didn't hunt or fish or watch sports or work on cars. And "Hey, did you guys watch *What Not to Wear?*" doesn't cut it as a conversation starter. I was like so many men today, who are really just like women except for the fact that they like women. Not that I want to do a disservice to sensitive males by making them think being a man is about their hobbies rather than their character. You shot a deer in the woods. I shot a DVD special in Detroit. We can both be men.

When my wife married me, I was a man who didn't talk about money and felt okay with a woman supporting me. I thought I was progressive. I think that's what you call being a woman in a man's body anyway.

Husbands, let me ask you: Have you become an overly sensitive male?

Wives, does your husband need to be re-manned like I did?

Does he notice things like the liquid soap didn't come from Bath & Body Works? The only thing men should know about soap is that it's not Lava. And if you don't know that Lava is a soap brand, just take your hand lotion and go home.

I say all this as a man who was not being a man. That's why I get a little preachy about all this man stuff.

I like what my friend Sean Cullum says: "I used to be vegetarian, but then I noticed . . . I was a man."

There used to be a time when you could talk straight to men, meaning you could be blunt and not worry about them pouting. Man up, men, take responsibility for your offspring and families, or call yourselves something other than men. Call yourselves the Other Kind of Women or Men Minus or Tall Boys or Ken Dolls, but something other than men.

I say all this as a man who was not being a man. That's why I get a little preachy about all this man stuff. I was not taking responsibility. I was depending on my wife the way I had depended on my mom.

I've made a six-figure income for the last several years. Yes, I can sense your sympathy building. Yet I have managed to save zero. So I did accomplish that. My wife matched my savings, and we combined them, but even that didn't seem to help.

My burden isn't debt.

It's regret.

This is where the bitterness comes in: My wife was in the corporate world before she became a stay-at-home mom. The temptation when you're struggling financially is to have her become a stay-at-work mom. When she worked in the corporate world, she was responsible for more than seventy people. She was accustomed to lots of responsibility, so when she became a stay-at-home mom she took over the finances. Being a stand-up comic, I was used to avoiding responsibility. There's something comforting about being the breadwinner and not having to worry about the bread.

Dinika: "Honey, we're short this month."

Me: "Hey, I don't keep the books."

Honestly, I was more than happy that she was responsible for all the bills because I've avoided responsibility my entire life. That's what comedians do. We make jokes. We don't face reality. Though I did make some suggestions, which allowed me to do nothing but shift the blame. You see the genius of my plan?

Do I blame my wife for our total money meltdown?

Yes. Of course.

What else am I going to do?

Take responsibility?

That's what makes it so comical. I blamed her for decisions that I never followed through on. It goes back to a guy who gets mad at his wife because he can't find something. Somehow men think that women should know where everything in the house is at any given moment.

> **Even now I'm amazed that my wife and I can talk about our finances.**

How should we deal with the bitterness?

I'll tell you as soon as I find my notes.

"Honey, what did you do with my notes?" Oh, that woman![3]

You can only do it if you're in it together. If you BOTH take responsibility and decide you want to climb out together. You know what needs to be done. If you want to lose weight, you stop eating so much. If you want to save money, you stop spending so much. If you want the government, the banks, and the Fed to take responsibility, you . . . well, there's nothing you can do about that.

Unfortunately, there is no Lap-Band for your wallet.

There are no fancy tricks.

Even now I'm amazed that my wife and I can talk about our finances. Sometimes. It's like running that potato sack race at the county fair. If you didn't happen to grow up in rural Nebraska, don't worry, I'm sure you've seen potato sack races in movies. The point is, both of you have one leg in a bag and you have to run together. Now, it doesn't help that you're being chased by creditors who are running bagless, but you can only do it together. You'll have to talk about money together.

Not yell.

My biggest breakthrough in taking responsibility happened when Dinika spoke to her multimillionaire brother about our financial situation.

My brother-in-law Paul designed some kind of computer chip, started a company in Silicon Valley, and sold it. Now he just works to keep from being bored. He's a caring brother who offered her $8,000 to keep us afloat. I felt utter humiliation, which is just a notch above complete humiliation. My wife was just looking for a way to help our family. Not that it wasn't a kind gesture, but borrowing money from relatives will ensure that one of you never shows up for Thanksgiving dinner again. And sharing your financial woes with someone other than your spouse without their consent will make your spouse feel discouraged and deflated, close cousins to humiliated. Boy, did I want to take that money. But saying no was a first step in taking responsibility.

At some point, you have to admit: It's my fault.

Now send me your address because I have some bills that you're to blame for.

WHO NOT TO PAY WHEN YOU'RE OUT OF MONEY
(Otherwise Known as a Budget)

....

This month it looks so bleak that I think it is going to be the first month that we miss our mortgage payment. One high-paying gig for the month cancelled today, the week before I was to be there. That's the money we budgeted for our mortgage payment. I have another gig next week for a pastor friend, which means it's cut-rate, so I'm not getting paid my standard honorarium. I have a great event at the end of the month, but it comes at the very end of the month, and we are honestly out of money now.

It looks bleak.

We are broke.

This seems like the perfect time to do a family devotional on fasting.

My poor wife is completely down in the dumps. "Maybe we should declare bankruptcy," she said with a trace of defeat in her voice, standing outside the second-story window ledge. Yeah, now that we're broke we can't hire anyone to clean the windows.

Two of our closest friends declared bankruptcy and, of course, that taught us a great lesson: Sometimes bankruptcy works out. They appear much better off two years later. I'm not encouraging bankruptcy. All I'm saying is that it worked out for them. Don't look at me. They're the ones encouraging bankruptcy.

"That's so encouraging, honey," I said.

"How's bankruptcy encouraging?"

"Well, look at it this way. We're broke, not bankrupt. It could be worse."

"Yeah, I guess. By the way, we're tithing a pound of Morton's salt this Sunday."

Now we have to sit down and figure out who not to pay.

This is called a budget.

I hate budgets. It's depressing figuring out how much you owe to whom and then figuring out that you don't have enough to pay them all. You get to the point where you have to put a stop-payment on a check so you can have a birthday party for a family member. Thanks, honey, it was a great surprise party! The biggest surprise was that we didn't have enough to cover the cake. You might think I'm only saying that to make a joke, but it's the sad truth. My wife threw me a birthday party and actually had to do this. That's how bleak our situation got—we were upside-down on a birthday cake. (You can make your own pineapple joke.)

I have what is called an irregular income, but somehow Macy's doesn't care. They want regular payments from my irregular income. Instead of Macy's, we should have applied for a card at an irregular clothing store. So my sleeves aren't the same length. So what? At least they don't expect regular payments.

Detailed budgets aren't for everyone, if by "everyone" you mean me. Maybe you just have to get used to feeling depressed every time you look at your budget. My wife and I handled things a bit differently, but we'll get to that.

Dave Ramsey has created helpful worksheets to help you budget your money, such as the Debt Snowball, a form that you use to list your debts from least depressing to most depressing. This is easy to fill out. We have records of our debt. We call them records. Our creditors call them bills. Picky, picky, picky. And they want them paid on time. Picky, picky, picky. I only wish it really was a debt snowball because we live in Southern California and I'd like to sit and watch that puppy melt.

This morning we sat down for breakfast, hot waffles and syrup, and decided to fill out the Monthly Cash-flow Plan, which is especially difficult to fill out when there is no cash to flow. My suggestion, before you embark upon any plan, is to pray with your spouse before you begin this process, because you'll come to a line like

Like it or not, you're going to have to make a list of everyone you owe. (I just hope you paid cash for this book.)

"tires" and ask your wife, "How much are tires for the car?" And she won't know. But somehow, since she was the one buying tires in the past, you'll feel like she's being evasive because it's about money. So you'll say, "When you want to know something, you know it, and when you don't want to know, you don't."

Then she'll say, "You're calling me a know-it-all."

"No, I'm not. I'm calling you a conditional know-it-all."

And then you'll have an extra monthly bill to remove the syrup stain from your shirt.

But you need to figure out who to pay.

Like it or not, you're going to have to make a list of everyone you owe. (I just hope you paid cash for this book.) Things like mortgage or rent payments, car payments, parking expenses, credit card payments, student loan payments, electric, gas, water, Internet, cell phone, health insurance, auto insurance, life insurance, and so on. And on.

The first thing you'll notice about this list is that you live an incredibly boring life. Who knew it was so expensive to be boring?

Budgeting is hard for us to do because of my irregular income. It's hard to create a budget based on hope.

"We need to make the mortgage payment."

"Well, let's hope I get a gig."

So, I made copies of all the forms that came in Dave's book. Then I followed the next step, which was to lose them. Who uses hard copies these days? I tracked things for four months. It was depressing because I'd been doubling up on some payments, paying twice the due amount, but after the interest it was like paying half of what I doubled up on. What? These credit cards are tricky. But it's not just our credit cards, which number twelve. There are two hospital bills, a dental bill, BillMeLater, which bills me now and later, and a few other stragglers. It's all there on the sheet.

What isn't on the sheet is the emotional cost of being in debt. Each one of these sheets forges a chain of worry and regret that is tethered to my neck (think of creepy, creeping Jacob Marley in *A Christmas Carol*). It's like my tie is too tight, which is odd because I don't wear ties. Our strides are slower, not bouncy like those of carefree people. This is the point where we are most tempted to give up. This is where we say something like, "This plan doesn't seem realistic." We say this because we feel the chains of debt tethered to our neck, which I mistake as fashion accesories. They're not real, but I feel them. Our mortgage is due.

I'm not sure Dave is going to want to hear this, but I stopped monitoring the sheets after the sixth month. That's not to say we gave up a budget. This is where I took a detour from the standard advice given by most financial advisors. It's the only place where I detoured from Dave's plan. Forgive me, Dave.

Here's my variation on budgets and how I've come to terms with them.

Budgets are like diets. Some people need Weight Watchers. They need to eat breakfast and then run to the computer to keep tab of their points for the day. And they do this every meal, which is fine. For obsessive-compulsive people. It works for them. They lose weight.

Other people just decide to eat less. That's all. And they lose weight.

That's my variation on the detailed budget. We buy less junk. We spend less. We stopped charging things, which is like giving up sugar.

We buy cereal that's in plastic bags instead of boxes. That's about the gist of it—spend less, pay out more until all your debt is gone. Google "frugal." That'll help clarify things.

Honestly, we don't really budget my income. At the moment, we budget my paychecks.

"We have some money. What do we need to spend it on right now? Would you like water and heat?"

"Good choice, honey. Write another check."

"What about health insurance?"

"How much is it again?"

"Seven hundred dollars a month."

"I feel pretty good. How about you?"

This phrase "being upside-down on your home loan" really paints a vivid picture, because that's how it feels.

At this point our mortgage payment is a luxury item.

This phrase "being upside-down on your home loan" really paints a vivid picture, because that's how it feels. It's like our home is trying to flip, the rooftop turning toward the ground, the ground floor reaching for the sky, while I'm in the doorway trying to keep it stable. Trying to keep it level. Trying to maintain it.

Things are not working out.

But then I get a call about doing a commercial for Ashley Furniture Home Stores. On top of that, I get a call for a last-minute gig for Saturday. Both of these gigs are sandwiched on either side of my cut-rate gig.

Thankfully, God provided everything right on time.

Again.

Now, this isn't to say that you just sit back and presume God will take care of everything. That's presumptuous, thus my use of the word "presume" in the previous sentence. The point is to find out what type of budgeting works best for you. Do you need a detailed budget? Can you get by with a general mind-set of spend less, pay out more?

My suggestion is to get completely out of debt and then fill out all these forms. That would be encouraging.

For once.

PART TWO:

_____

MONEY AND YOUR HABITS

(or the Necessity of Starbucks)

_____

YOUR PAST HOLDS THE KEY TO YOUR FINANCES

(But Your Family Lost the Key and the Cash Box It Opened)

....

M y parents never talked about money. They screamed about money. They nagged about money, but they never talked about money. Nagging about money is just as bad as fighting about money. It really has the same effect on the kids, who say to themselves, *Man, I'm never going to talk about money with anyone because all you do is fight about it. I'll just deny it exists.*

Then you grow up, bring all this financial baggage from your past with you, and marry someone under the assumption that they have a better set of luggage. Our formative years have a substantial influence on the lives we lead. We might as well blame our parents for being broke, too. That's a joke, Mom. But looking at our past can help us understand why we think about money the way we do.

Some of our money habits were learned from our families, which is what makes personal finances personal. When two people join in holy matrimony, they bring a collective financial history with them. Well, in our case, *collective* is the wrong word. The only thing we collected was debt. In this respect, my wife and I have always been a perfect match: We both believed in spending money. Until debt do us part.

One of my earliest memories of moola is about a special lunch program that my mother wanted me to join. It was third grade, and my father was having heart problems, so finances were as short as my pop's breath. Mom wanted to sign me up for some program where I could get free lunches. But to get the free lunch, you had to line up with all the other kids who received free lunches, like the freakishly tall kid whose pants buttoned at his chest. I still have his photo. Hey, wait a second. That's me! Cue snare drum.

When I was a kid, every day before school my mother would give me "milk money," which was money that I used to buy candy with after school.

This was a small town, rural Nebraska potato-sack-racing land, so it was only about six or seven kids, but it was six or seven kids I didn't want to eat lunch with. Taking my mother up on her policy of "you can tell me anything," I told her that I didn't want to get free lunches, and I told her why—I might catch the cooties. I was embarrassed by the idea of getting a handout. But with his heart condition, my dad's income had suffered because he couldn't work the same hours, which according to Mom were "more hours than there are in a day." That's a lot of overtime. Mom told me that I didn't have to take the free lunches.

Even after the free lunch crisis, I still never had the impression we were poor. I was sheltered from the shame of being one of the free-lunch kids, who all dressed like they were poor and were unpopular with the other kids. No one has to know you're poor if you spend all your money on the right clothes. It's something we all understand from a young age: money is about image. Keep a good one. That's the first money lesson I learned well. I always had nice clothes.

When I was a kid, every day before school my mother would give me "milk money," which was money that I used to buy candy with after school. Got milk? No, I got candy! It was money budgeted for milk, but I spent it on candy. That's the second money lesson I learned well. Don't use it for what it's intended; use it for something that tastes good, like the Dish NFL package.

But it was the homemade bike that did me in.

All the other kids in my neighborhood were peddling around on Schwinn Apple Krates and Orange Krates, the popular brand-name bikes of the day. I think it was all of them. It's hard to tell when you're riding your bike around with a paper bag over your head. The Apple Krate bike was a flamboyant red (the official name of the color) and came with a banana seat, a five-speed Stik-Shift, a MAG sprocket (I prefer Spacely's, where George Jetson works), and Sting-Ray handlebars, but its front tire was small, like that of a chopper motorcycle. They were the coolest bikes around. So, naturally, I didn't have one.

The Apple Krate kids would park their bikes in a row at the baseball park, a display of what the rest of us didn't have—rides to the game. I remember clearly they were Schwinn bicycles, because they had logos. This logo meant "cool." Those kids with bikes from Sears couldn't compete. We were kids, but we knew the score. Logos meant something. Schwinn stood for quality while Sears stood for cheap parents. My homemade bike stood for "My dad grew up during the Depression."

Depression-era bikes do not have logos.

While all my friends showed off their new bikes, mine was made by my father, who loved to create mechanical oddities like lamps made out of driftwood so we could swim at night, and coffee tables made out of wagon wheels that would rotate the dip. So, when I asked for a new bike, he informed me that he would build me one. He spent as much money on the new seat and handlebars and tires and pedals as he would have spent on a new bike. But it wasn't new. It was a spray-painted old frame with new parts. It was unique, I'll give it that. How many bikes have a chip dip holder?

I just wanted a bike like everyone else. A bike with a logo, instead of a homemade bike. And there was no spray paint with sparkles in it, so my bike had a dull, matte finish.

I was determined that things would be different when I got older.

When I became an adult, I wanted everything to be new and brand name. It took years to appreciate the quaintness of vintage. Not that I want our vintage to actually be vintage. I'd rather pay for something brand-new that was made to look vintage. Initially, our search for vintage-looking kitchen cabinets began at Home Depot. Then we had "an appointment" with a kitchen designer who wasn't part of a warehouse chain store. She was with a "specialty" store. You see? We wanted our kitchen to be special. And it is. Three times as special as a Home Depot kitchen. People walk in and "ooh and aah" and can't find the fridge because it looks like part of the cabinetry.

That's worth three times the special.

To this day, I've never bought anything off Craigslist, America's Internet garage sale. My wife buys stuff from there all the time. Before we had our second child, when the money was flowing and the economy was booming, I would always say, "I'm not gonna have my kid playin' with that secondhand stuff." And I'd go out and buy a new Playskool large plastic house, because toddler real estate prices hadn't gone bust yet. Thanks to Craigslist, kids are flipping Playskool homes.

Our second child's toys are all from Craigslist. Little Kate Tulip is only two-years-old, but she'll soon be able to recognize name brands, distinguishing old things from new things. She knows who Elmo is, and she loves him, which makes me feel a little better, because he looks second hand already.

Dinika and I have similar financial backgrounds, which means that neither one of us married for money. Her father was a choral music teacher, and my pop had his own small trucking company, but he hummed between deliveries. Now you may assume that my dad could beat up her dad, but her dad taught choral music in Saudi Arabia for over a decade. This made him the Clint Eastwood of choral directors. "Get off my sand." As a choral music teacher in Saudi Arabia, he made the same wages as a doctor in America. And since there is nothing to do in Saudi Arabia but save money, he saved a ton of money. The trouble was, my wife didn't live with her father growing up, so the only financial lesson she learned from her dad was that, to save money, you had to leave the country.

Another thing I remember vividly about money while I was growing up is that my mother didn't like how my dad managed his business. She was always complaining about a customer who owed him money that he wasn't collecting quickly enough. However, to my dad, the people he did business with were his friends, so he'd let them slide. Mom resented this. I think. Maybe she smashed the dishes because she just didn't like the floral pattern around the edges, but this combination taught me to avoid talking about money at all costs. Because you can't have cookies and milk when all the cups are broken.

Maybe that's why I struggle with talking about the simplest money matters. Like today, I returned some antislide coasters for our couch to Home Depot while my wife waited in the car with the kids. Home Depot gave me cash, nearly seven whole dollars. Now, I returned these coasters because they didn't work. The mission was to find some that did work so we could sit on the couch without needing a travel agent. You know. It slides across the room. Wood floors. So I find some other rubber grip pads to set the couch on that are only four bucks, and I use our debit card to pay for them. (No more credit cards, right Dave?)

Well, I put the seven bucks in my wallet so I could have a guilt-free trip to Starbucks, meaning that my wife wouldn't see it on our online bank account, which tells all. I should probably give up Starbucks altogether, but Dave hasn't mentioned that yet. He just said cut up all your credit cards. The rule is if you can pay cash for Starbucks, you can have some. But daily? I probably spend about $150 a month on Starbucks.

I'm certain I'll tell my wife all of this before she reads it. Show her the advance check the publisher gave me. Buy her a Starbucks. Then tell her. That's a good rule: Anytime you have to confess something to your wife, buy her a Starbucks first. Caffeine makes people forgive faster. Right? Speeds things up.

Get her a drink that's swirly.

Do you find yourself doing things like this because you fear it might lead to an argument about money?

Oh, you don't.

Oh.

Awkard silence.

I never felt deprived of anything as a kid, besides a logo for my bike. But I never thought we were rich, either. We did live in a big house, but it was an old house, so it didn't qualify as a rich person's house to me. That's why this whole American Dream is very relative. In grade school, one of the kids commented about not being "rich like you. We don't live in a big, old house." To him, "rich" equaled the size of your home. To me, "rich" equaled "new." After buying our first home I was disappointed that it didn't come with a logo.

You can get a glimpse of your financial future by looking at your parents. Now, if that doesn't rattle your financial cage with fright that knocks your change together, nothing will.

Even though my grandpa was an accountant, I don't think my mother balanced a checkbook until my dad passed away. However, she always championed savings. Not that I had a personal savings account growing up, but I was always told it was a good idea. But there was this underlying philosophy that you had to be rich to save money. We didn't have the extra money rich people had; all our money was sitting uncollected in the wallets of Dad's friends.

My wife's mother was originally a member of Hollywood's elite, the daughter of an MGM prop master, who worked on the *Wizard of Oz* among other films while she herself frolicked around the back lot with child actors like Margaret O'Brien, Dean Stanton, and Robert Blake. She married into the lower showbiz rung of Saudi Arabian choral music directors, but she never stopped spending money like she was from Hollywood's elite.

That pretty much summed up our view of money. We spent money like we were rich. And to some people, we are rich. This makes our former spending habits all the worse.

You can get a glimpse of your financial future by looking at your parents. Now, if that doesn't rattle your financial cage with fright that knocks your change together, nothing will. Do you want that kind of financial future?

I know a young newly married woman who grew up in a financially well-to-do but unstable home. Her father made a lot of money, so they spent a lot of money. And in spending so much, her parents always fought about money. This young woman decided that would not be her future. Thus, she became a financial miser, even resentful of tithing to the point that her husband has to write the checks for church as long as he can find where she hid the checkbook. She can't bring herself to give money away.

The problem with this kind of overcorrection is that it's behavior modification and not heart-driven change. If she doesn't cooperate with God and develop a generous heart, then she will likely propagate the reverse problem in her children. As adults, her children will complain, "My mother was such a miser we couldn't buy anything new. We couldn't buy anything old. So now we buy whatever we want." Her children will become her parents. Now, that might be sweet revenge for Grandpa and Grandma, but that's what can happen when we don't see our finances as an issue of the heart.

Unless we become aware of how our financial past has shaped us, we might be doomed to repeat it or swing the opposite dysfunctional direction. Even now, I have to admit that the name Schwinn doesn't mean the same thing it did to me as a kid. When I was a kid it meant cool. Now it just means I wasn't allowed to have cool things as a kid. What a horribly relative association brand names can be.

Ultimately, we can't really blame our parents for our bad financial decisions. At least not in print. Sure, parents can play a large role in training up their children in wise ways, but we children have to eventually decide to walk in those wise ways. Even if our parents didn't train us wisely, the wisdom is out there if we truly seek it. (See the book of Proverbs.) Many of us think our lives would not only be better if our parents had trained us better, but we think that our lives would be better if our parents were wealthy and gave us a stack of James Madisons.[4]

I know this much: speculation will not get us out of debt.

My wife and I realized that before we could begin any financial turn-around, we both had to want a financial turnaround from the heart, not just a reactionary emotional response to the way we were raised. Couples need to agree that it's about changing their hearts. If one is moving forward and the other is moving backward, well . . . do the math . . . you can't ride a tandem bike that way. I don't care if it is a Schwinn.

Sit down (fore to aft), agree that you're in a mess, and ask God to change your hearts.

Now, begin pedaling.

MONEY MYTHS
(The First One Being That I Have Any)

....

M y wife and I walked by a BMW convertible, and I commented, "That's a cool-looking car."

"That's a midlife crisis car," she said.

"Man, I sure hope I can afford a midlife crisis."

"It's a little late for that."

"I'm not that old," I said.

"I thought we were past the denial stage," she said.

Little did I know how much that statement revealed my faulty financial thinking. I was hoping things would work out instead of having to formulate a financial plan and implementing it. We had no financial plan. Shoot. We have no dental plan. I am a self-employed stand-up comedian and writer. My dental plan is—chew on the side that doesn't hurt. It's a two-part plan: plan A, the right cheek, plan B, the left cheek.

Choose one.

One of the dumbest things we believed about ourselves was that we were good with money because we paid our bills on time. The fact that we had bills shows that we were not good with money. Rich people don't have bills. They have money, which I believe is the key to being rich.

One of the clues to our bleak financial future was how I handled paying the bills in our early marriage. Such as the day my wife called me up on my cell phone and said, "Yeah, I just wanted you to know I can't call you from home because the phone's been disconnected."

"Hmmm. They disconnected our phone?"

Hmmm, I was very surprised. I was amazed that they would shut off our phone. I mean, we have the money to pay them. It's in the bank. So what could it be? It sounds like a conspiracy to me. I mean, is it personal? They just don't care for me?

"Honey, I don't understand. Why would they shut off our phone?"

My wife was like, "Well, let me explain it to you, Peach. The money that we have in *our* bank? They want it in *their* bank. We need to send it to their bank. And when *you* don't send them *our* money from *our* bank, *they* shut off the phone."

"All of 'em?"

"Yeah, all of them."

I thought maybe they might just punish us. Shut off a few phones. You know, shut off the phones downstairs. Make us run upstairs for everything.

I believed some really dumb things about money. Shoot. I believed commercials where they offered "90 days same as cash," which doesn't really work out that way. Pull three pages from your calendar, and then go to your local bank and try to exchange them for cash. You can even show them the advertisement that proclaims "90 days same as cash," and they still won't give you any money.

Take it from me, if you want to recover financially, you have to stop believing dumb things about money.

The first dumb thing we need to stop believing about money is that we'll get better about handling money *in the future*. I remember seeing a Dave Ramsey book fifteen years ago and thinking, "That would probably be good to read." But we were newly married, so I didn't want to spend the cash on a book about cash. There were restaurants to go to. I always meant to read it and I finally got around to fifteen years later. I don't know who coined the phrase "Better late than never," but he was stupid. "Better late" is California time. Later is never better. Later will

"Money's not important?" Only a young Christian with no money could hold such a naive view.

cost you millions of dollars. Had I followed Dave's advice fifteen years ago, I could be a millionaire today instead of a funny poor man.

The second dumb thing we need to stop believing is that money is not spiritual enough. As a new Christian, I didn't think a book about money was spiritual enough to read. I wanted to grow as a Christian, not as a financial wizard. Money's not important. "Money's not important?" Only a young Christian with no money could hold such a naive view. People marry for money. People divorce for money. People stay single for money. Countries go to war for money. Companies exist to make money. Churches exist because of money. Missionaries spread the gospel with money. Money allows you to enjoy a leisurely afternoon. Money enables you to root for your favorite sport. Money is why books are published. Money is why art is sold. Money is why some legislation passes and some fails. Money makes the world go round. That's right. There's a rotation fee.

I nearly titled this book *Money Is the Answer for Everything (Unless You Don't Have Any),* because that's what the Bible says. Well, the part in parentheses is mine, but King Solomon did write in Ecclesiastes that "money is the answer for everything."[5] Now, whether he meant this tongue-in-cheek or not, the point remains clear. Money is important. Think of something you'd like to do. Anything. I bet it's going to cost you some money. Money is vital. Oddly, some of us Christians who aren't prosperity-driven fail to realize this.

Money is vital because God thinks it's vital.

Money is mentioned about 800 times in the Bible—that's more than

2,300 verses on the theme of money and possessions alone. That's twice as many verses as there are on faith and prayer combined, because when you don't have any money, you spend more time praying about it. Fifteen percent of Jesus' teachings are related to the topic of money, and that's more than His teachings on heaven and hell combined. Now there's a sermon series I'd like to hear: "Bankers in the Hands of an Angry God." Or "Heaven, Hell, and Interest Only."

In the parable of the talents, Jesus tells us a story about a man who entrusts his servants with talents—a type of currency in that day—as he sees fit. Some biblical scholars estimate that a talent was worth twenty years of wages, a standard Hollywood has kept to this day. If we convert that to our day, with the average income being $45,000, that's . . . not that math is my strong suit . . . something just under a million dollars. That's a lot of talent. This guy was a generous master.

Now we tend to spiritualize this parable (because it is about the kingdom of God), but it's still about investing money. Why do we think that's not spiritual? Because it's money? It's obviously spiritual if we only remember that Jesus said, "For where your treasure is, there your heart will be also."[6] Our checkbooks leave a trail of what's really important to us. If you're curious about your spiritual state, take a gander at your checkbook. There is a clear link between our spiritual lives and how we spend our money. One tells us about the other.

What's in your wallet?

Heaven or hell?

The third dumb thing we need to stop believing about money is that it's ours. All things are from Christ and through Christ and to Christ. When you tithe, you're not giving money to God. You just get to keep some. That's all. It's all God's. Everything. Our money, our homes, our talents, our children, our time, everything. "The earth is the Lord's, and everything in it."[7] Everything is His, so you'd think we'd be better about tithing. We're just stewards, which means "neighbors who borrowed the rake."

Proverbs 3:9–10 (ESV) says, "Honor the Lord with your wealth and with the firstfruits of all your produce; then your barns will be filled with plenty, and your vats will be bursting with wine." So there is a promise that God will abundantly provide for us if we handle our money properly. All *you* have to do is go out and get yourself a vat. Interestingly, right after these verses comes, "My son, do not despise the Lord's discipline or be weary of his reproof, for the Lord reproves him whom he loves, as a father the son in whom he delights." And sometimes that's what I feel this whole book is about. God is lovingly teaching me right views of money and wealth, but it took discipline for me to get it.

When we were first married, my car was such a piece of junk that my wife wouldn't fill it up because she feared the car wouldn't outlast a tank of gas.

My new viewpoint is that preachers don't talk about money nearly enough. They might beg for it too much, but they don't talk about it enough. When we complain that all preachers do is talk about money, it's probably because we don't want to give any of our money away. Sure, the prosperity guys and gals distort God's gracious teaching on provision, but that's no excuse to avoid teaching about money. That's why we should be teaching about it all the more.

Our giving isn't based on getting. It's based on gratitude for a God who freely gave us His Son and then asks us, "How will he not also, along with him, graciously give us all things?"[8] Because God graciously gave to us, we graciously give back. That's how the gospel affects our giving. We don't give to get. We give to give. If we only give to get, then we're like a husband who builds his wife a gazebo on Saturday morning, but only because Saturday morning means there'll be a Saturday night. (Now some guys might feel like building a gazebo is a little overboard, but they haven't seen my wife.)

The fourth dumb thing we need to stop believing about money is that we need a car payment to drive a reliable car. This is the mother of all dumb things to believe about money. I've driven my share of clunkers. There is a term to describe people who spend so much money on car repairs that they are suicidal—mechanic depressive. You ever call your car a piece of junk and then end up apologizing to your car? Patting the dash and pleading, "I'm sorry. You're a good car. Please, please, if you start—I'll replace the garbage bag with a real window."

When we were first married, my car was such a piece of junk that my wife wouldn't fill it up because she feared the car wouldn't outlast a tank of gas.

Then the economy turned around, and someone gave me a car loan, something I had trouble getting in the past as a self-employed stand-up comedian. Living in Chicago, having abandoned my brush-painted orange Volvo on the side of the interstate, I walked four blocks to a local Mazda dealership and they gave me a loan. I didn't even lie on the application. That's how good the economy was at the time. They were just passing out loans to stand-up comedians.

I barely qualified to drive a car, let alone have a loan on one.

Most of us buy cars we don't even need, like new ones.

Be still, my child. One of the biggest ways to waste your money is that car payment you deem so necessary. It's not. Please. Be still, my child.

My wife and I just made our last car payment.

Immediately after paying off this car, the temptation was to get a second car because we're a one-car family. My wife has to drive me to the airport and pick me up. I always have to leave before the coffee at Starbucks is even finished brewing, and we have two kids who have to get up and ride along. It's very easy to make a second car sound justifiable.

But the car is paid for now.

Click.

The last payment. (That was the sound of my mouse, not the phone. We pay our bills online.)

Whenever you make the last payment for something online, I think the bank's website should play a little celebration tune for you. But it doesn't. It's just "click"—the-car's-paid-for-now.

One of our best friends said, "Isn't that a great feeling?"

"No," I said. "It's not. Because we still made a payment. Talk to me next month when we don't have to make a payment. That will be a great feeling."

These days I'm happy to drive a clunker, not that our 2006 Dodge Magnum is a clunker. I'm just happy to drive anything that's paid off. Oddly enough, as soon as a car is paid off, it becomes a clunker. The timing of the auto industry is impeccable.

It's time to dispel the myth about that new car smell. Want to know what that new car smell really is? Fresh debt. Mmmmm, what a sweet aroma.

Besides, clunkers are safer.

While I was out of town, my wife was carjacked in our own driveway. On the bright side, at least she didn't have far to walk home. The car salesperson didn't happen to mention to us that the Dodge Magnum we purchased is one of the top three carjacked cars in the country. We thought we were buying a station wagon, but no. We bought a getaway car. Our bad.

The carjackers followed her home from the grocery store. Two of the future inmates ambushed her in the driveway. Initially, the dude holding the handgun asked her for her purse. Then the older dude asked for the car keys. The younger dude asked, "Whatta ya doin'?" And the older dude said, "Get in the car," not to my wife but to the younger gang member. The gang member plebe said, "Sorry, ma'am," to my wife, which I'm sure the judge will take into consideration.

"How do you plead?"

"Guilty. But I said I was sorry."

Then they were gone, followed by the car that dropped them off in front of the house. There were three suspects involved in taking a purse away from a suburban homemaker. It took three men to handle my wife.

For some reason, one of the gang members felt compelled to use my wife's cell phone and call the last person she spoke with, who happened to be me. I was sitting in a movie theater in Nashville, Tennessee, when my phone vibrated. Thankfully, it was such a boring movie that I was looking for any excuse to walk out. So I took the call, thinking it was Dinika because it was her name on the screen.

"Hey, Peach!"

All I heard was cussing on the other end of the line.

"Did I forget to take out the trash before I left?"

This gang member did not take kindly to being called "Peach."

After a few more verbal assaults, he hung up.

As you can imagine, I was panicked with worry. He might make a long-distance call! Okay, my real concern was, "Where's my wife?"

She was being interviewed by a local detective who shared many things that frightened her even more—like the one about the carjackers who had recently been taking not only the cars but also the people, driving them out to a remote location, shooting the owners of the autos in the head, and then moving on with the car. The detective was just there to help.

When the detective asked my wife, What did they look like? she said, A gun. They looked like a gun. Because when someone is pointing a gun at you, that's what you look at. So, you have to ask yourself, "Is that new car worth it?"

Pay cash for an older car.

It just might save your life.

LITTLE THINGS ADD UP
(So Do Big Things—but I Can't Afford Those)

....

Starbucks is my happy place, my first romance with corporate America. My local Starbucks baristas know me by drink. They look at me when I walk in and say, "Venti iced chai? Seven pumps?" This is why I love Starbucks. They always make me feel welcome. I walk in, and a barista asks with a big smile, "How are you today?"

"Well, I'm better now that you made me feel welcome."

I don't even care that it's a corporate policy smile. I'll take it. "Thanks for reading the company manual." The baristas always put me in a better mood. Just say the word "barista" aloud. It's a very happy word. It's not just iced chai tea. It's iced chai tea and someone who's paid to be glad to see me. That's worth $5.90 a day. (You may have to adjust this joke for inflation.)

Here's my problem: Part of the reason I barely have enough to pay my fixed expenses is that I'm spending a lot of money on items that aren't necessities at all.

Starbucks is a prime example. You could say Starbucks is one of my greatest weaknesses. Or it's one of my greatest strengths, depending on your view of caffeine. I have such a love for the place that I'd rather quit paying the utility bill than go without Starbucks. Most of us view heat in our homes as a necessity when that's not the case at all. Heat only makes it easier to sleep. It's not necessary. Wouldn't you like to see more babies born? Get rid of heat in your home, and your spouse will finally snuggle the way you've always dreamed.

Starbucks is another story. I can live without heat. Starbucks has hot drinks.

The atmosphere is one draw for me. The soothing green color calms jittery coffee drinkers. It invites you back, the warm wood and folksy faux-chalkboard specials and padded chairs and smart-looking people with glasses showing off their Apple products. Plus, the tables are never sticky. They wipe their tables off. That always brings me back.

I'm a gold card member, which is basically a frequent-drinking program. My average is $150 a month, and with every fifteen purchases I get a free drink. Congratulations. That's thirty drinks a month, which is two free drinks each month. Subtract the savings, and I only spend $140 a month at Starbucks.

But who's really counting? Besides the accountants at Starbucks. Yeah, I have a problem, and I don't even drink coffee. I drink chai tea and eat pastries, specifically low-fat cinnamon swirl coffee cake. It's low-fat. And it's swirly. Did you hear me? It's swirly.

Don't judge me.

It's swirly.

Besides, I paid cash today with the seven dollars Home Depot gave me from that return.

I'll have to cut back. Cash. Maybe $50 a month. Maybe I can sell something around the house. Maybe we can have a monthly garage sale to supply my Starbucks habit. If it's not in the budget, you have to figure out other ways. A lemonade stand maybe?

The truth is, little things like Starbucks add up. This is not news to you. I'll tell you what is news—have a chat with your local Starbucks barista about people's financial habits at Starbucks.

"How many people like me come in here daily?" I asked my barista.

"Oh, you don't want to know," she said.

So, there's Starbucks' financial policy—bury your head in the coffee.

"Twenty? Thirty?" I said.

"Hundreds."

Some customers come in two or three times a day, she told me. I know. I know. Their savings are really adding up. That's more like five free drinks each month. These people are saving nearly $25 a month. If I went in more than once a day, I could save more money, too. The more you buy, the more you save. That's Marketing 101. Wait a second. Marketing is about getting my money. Hey!

The crew (now every employee was involved in my financial survey) told me about one customer who orders eight black teas daily. She calls ahead and then comes in and picks up the order, which is $18 (with a $2 tip). That's . . . carry the one . . . I don't know . . . more than I spend there daily. This person is a really poor financial planner. If she just drank seven more black teas a day, she could get a free drink every day. Think of the savings.

> **Dave Ramsey says it more than once: "Personal finances is 80 percent behavior." And behavior is 100 percent your heart.**

Dave Ramsey says it more than once: "Personal finances is 80 percent behavior." And behavior is 100 percent your heart. For out of the heart come evil thoughts and $150 a month for caffeine fixes.

$150 a month at Starbucks is not good behavior.

Little things add up.

Maybe you don't eat out at expensive restaurants, but you eat out at so many little dives that you might as well eat out at expensive restaurants. Little things add up. What about ATM fees? What about bottled water? It's America. You can drink safely from a hose. Speaking of hoses, that's what you can wash your car with and save that little expense. How much do you spend on music every year? If you want to save money, talk to some twelve-year-old, and you'll be directed to a website where you can listen to music for free. What about energy drinks and fast food and cigarettes, the little things that slowly kill you? The procrastinator's guide to suicide.

When it comes to money, there are no little things. When it comes to life, there are no little things. Everything counts, and counting leads to addition, and addition leads to writing someone a check.

If my wife blew $150 this month on various things, which she did because, as she told me, "I spent twenty dollars on this various thing at Target today," then together we blew three hundred dollars this month. That's a part-time job at Starbucks. If we just gave up Starbucks, it would be like getting a part-time job at Starbucks.

That's $3,600 per year we can save.

Wow.

That doesn't even include the low-fat cinnamon swirl coffee cake, valued at $1,200 per year.

The point is . . . little things add up.

Big things add up too, but I can't afford them.

Like most Americans, we medicate with money. Feeling down? Let's go buy some new lawn furniture for the backyard. We don't have a drug problem or a drinking problem. We have a shopping problem. Bored? How about some new curtains for the living room? Like any good twelve-step program, you have to call upon a higher power to help you overcome years of decorative, I mean, destructive behavior.

When you're self-employed, you really notice little things like, oh, recessions. When a recession hits, the giving in churches drops even more than usual. When giving drops, there are no extra funds for special events like that workers' and leaders' appreciation banquet where they bring in a comedian to entertain the group. I'm a special event. So you notice the money's just not there to spend anymore, which is problematic for people who spend tons money.

"Let's invite some people over for dinner."

"And feed them what?"

"Oh, I see. You forgot to have the heat shut off."

"It was heat or eat, Babe."

My wife and I reinforce each other's bad spending habits. No one in our home goes to Target alone. This is why when your spouse begins making good financial decisions, you feel threatened. It's like the alcoholic who wants to stop drinking, but his drunk friend discourages him because he doesn't want to drink alone. That's American culture. No one wants to shop alone. You know you have a problem when you're hiding receipts and returns (see chapter 5).

Shopping is a way of life for us. In our minds, we aren't shopping. We are spending quality time together. At Target. The place where we have date night. My wife calls it, "The hundred-dollar store," because every time we go we spend no less than a hundred dollars on many little things.

"What kind of little things?" you ask.

Forgettable little things.

Toilet paper, cereal, some little toy plane that's also a sucker, seat pads for the kitchen chairs, Swedish Fish, a combination of necessities and useless-ities.

Eating out several times a week adds up, too. I travel a lot, so when I get home, my first thought is always about where we'll eat. It's my way of reconnecting with my family. Things are different in a money meltdown. Now I eat alone while they wait in the car. (That's a joke; they wait at home.)

Eating out might help me reconnect with my family, not to mention my old friend Pasta Milano, but there must be a way to reconnect that's not so expensive. "Let's try eating at home," I suggested. It was the oddest thing. As a family, we sat down at the dining room table and then—no one came to take our order. Dinnertime just isn't the same without food.

Those are just some of the ways little things add up.

If you find yourself discouraged, well, that shows you're right about how you've been handling money. Now all you have to do is trudge

> **When your heart begins to change, you will notice yourself saying no to unnecessary purchases more often.**

through the emotional pain of your personal financial habits.

It's not personal, it's credit.

One dime at a time.

When your heart begins to change, you will notice yourself saying no to unnecessary purchases more often. That's how I got my library card. My previous habit was to just buy whatever book I wanted at the time. It was always for research. And it's always good to read. Ironically, I often had to give many of the books to the library to make room on my bookshelf for more. We have tax receipts for all the books I bought last year. More than $1,500 worth of books. This year we saved that much by having a library card. Then we saved approximately $3,600 by not eating out as often. When we had two cars, I would drive myself to the airport, leave the car, and pay the parking fees. At twelve bucks a day, that added up $1,200 every year. Those are all little things we have since elminated, which has helped me keep my Starbucks habit.

Slowly, I'm changing the way I handle money.

I've started playing a little game called "The List of Little Things." When I want to buy something, but then say no to buying it, I make a mental note of it. For instance, I have this shower caddy that needs to be replaced. It holds my razor and toothbrush, so I can shave and brush in the shower. It's not sticking to the wall as well anymore and the mirror is corroded. Things like that drive me nuts. It's not that expensive, only twenty bucks. But I said to myself, "Be reasonable. You're the only one who sees it. It's not like guests are inspecting the upstairs bathroom." Now they don't have to. I just told them our shower caddy mirror is corroded.

Then I wanted a new pair of dress shoes. I have a pair and they're doing okay, but they're getting a little worn. But I asked myself, "Do they have holes in them? No. Are the heels in place? Yes. Well, buddy, you just saved yourself fifty dollars."

That's seventy bucks between the two.

Just keep saying no to little things you can get by without and then add up the savings.

It's just one of many ways you can eliminate Starbucks guilt.

The reason most of us start financial plans (and let's be honest, we've all started them . . . we just fail to finish them) is because we want to change the way we handle money. Then we see how badly we've handled money and grow discouraged. When we are discouraged, we quit.

Then we go to Starbucks to cheer ourselves up.

That's the plan, anyway.

IMAGINARY MONEY
(And Other Truths about Credit Cards)

....

My wife had plastic surgery. She cut up our credit cards. Cue snare drum. That's one of the reasons we stopped using them. Because my wife cut them to bits. She cut up the bills, too, but they kept sending new ones in the mail.

Credit cards allow us to fool ourselves. "One pretends to be rich, yet has nothing; another pretends to be poor, yet has great wealth."[9] We can pretend to be rich and yet have nothing. Well, nothing but 14 percent interest. That's something . . . if you're a loan shark. Loan sharks are from the olden days before banks took over their business by issuing credit cards. The difference between banks and loan sharks is that loan sharks used to break your legs if you didn't repay. Now, banks just break your credit, so you can't walk financially.

To help save us, my wife took scissors to the loan sharks of our lives. It was a simple but momentous moment. She stood over the trash and snipped them into the recycling bin. Half the card one day, half the next, to put the kibosh on any identity swipers good at jigsaw puzzles.

"How are we going to buy things now?" I asked.

"There's cash."

"I think I've seen that in movies."

Before that, we didn't notice our money melting away. Probably because we never really handled our money. I mean, we never really touched it. We had cards. Like most people, I have no problem spending imaginary money.

Imaginary money is credit card money. It's not like you're really spending money. No cash exchanges hands. If banks want to be fooled by this little plastic card, that's their problem. It's imaginary money, which they will soon find out when they try to collect it from me.

"But you charged this!"

"That doesn't mean I had any money. That's why I charged it. Because I don't have any money. If I had money, I wouldn't be charging things."

Silly banks.

When will we learn to stop using credit cards?

Today, I guess. Since my wife cut them up.

Here's an idea I like better than cutting up your credit cards. There is a company that sells a guitar pick punch. It's a handy little gadget that allows you to take something plastic, say like a credit card, and simply insert it, punch it, and voilà, you have guitar picks made out of your credit cards.[10]

We need to find another use for credit cards besides shopping.

James Scurlock writes in his scathing book *Maxed Out*, "The more people become dependent on credit, the more they need to keep going. Once Americans began using one credit card, for example, they tended to need another. And then another. And then higher credit limits. And then they needed to refinance their homes to pay off the credit card bills. And so on. No other product creates that cycle (well, crack and heroin come to mind, but . . .)."[11]

Please, take a moment right now and make a vow to God that you will never use a credit card again. Ever. Never. Never ever ever never.

Unless you play the guitar.

Credit is hard to say no to. Credit cards are always enticing us. The commercials pull at your emotional strings, ads written by credit card companies who want to remind you about what's "priceless" in life. They make you feel as warm and fuzzy as the slippers on your feet, even though you know the sham behind their sentiment. That's fake fuzz on the slippers. Other commercials make you feel like you're not protected without them, like a team of marauding Vikings is going to bust through your doors and repossess your furniture because of "what's in your wallet." The US Postal Service aids and abets these companies by sending us attractive offers in the mail, financial Valentines if you will.

Then there are the human beings in our lives, those significant relationships that make you feel like you're on top of the world—when really you're on top of the Dumpster—that you'll soon be sleeping in if you keep using credit cards.

Credit cards are evil. Not just standard evil, but "let's-fatten-up-the-children-and-eat-them" evil. If you use plastic, you pay 24 percent more for everything you buy, once you add up the interest these banks charge you. That's wicked-witch evil. It's Hansel-and-Gretel-are-on-the-milk-carton evil. But instead of Hansel and Gretel now it's Consumer and Credit.

Here's how banks use credit cards. First they leave a trail of bread crumbs that lead to the woods, which is where all people in debt hide. The bread crumbs are the letters you receive about preapproved credit and how special you are because you have pre-approved credit. You're very bright and special for having such a good credit rating, especially if you just graduated high school. And because you're so very bright and special, you're convinced that you, unlike all those other people, can handle the woods. Little do you know that all those trails in the woods are the fine print at the bottom of your credit agreement with the evil bank, but that's getting ahead of the story.

Late payments are the teeth banks use to bite you and gnash your bones.

You see a little bird singing that makes you forget about all your troubles, so you follow the little bird. The little bird is the credit card. Then you find the house made out of candy and gingerbread called the mall. Since you have the card you buy the house. And that's when they boil you and eat you.

Late payments are the teeth they use to bite you and gnash your bones. That's why you should never have a credit card to begin with. There are no rabies shots for Visa. Their late fees are like demons that are cast out and then bring back ten friends to enter your bill. The analogy goes like this: You pay on time, and you make a little dent, which is like casting a demon out. Then you're late on your $15.00 payment, and they charge you a $39 late fee plus whatever other fees. Emotional trauma fee for making the bank feel neglected. That $15.00 demon brings back four friends, and now you're paying over $50.00.

Pay on time (until you're debt free), and keep those demons at bay.

Thanks to one of my credit card companies, Large Nameless Generic Bank, I discovered just how powerless an individual American citizen truly is when it comes to dealing with the evil of consumer credit.

My story begins as a somewhat innocent (a gracious term to be sure—"blissfully ignorant" would also be accurate, or "intentionally ignorant" would be right on the money, so to speak) consumer who turns his mailbox key to behold "convenience checks" from Large Nameless Generic Bank. Convenience checks look like regular checks that your local bank sends you, except the printing at the top reads, "To Activate these checks, call 1-800-whatever." Not needing the checks, I tossed them in a drawer with other junk mail that I might need one day, like applications for other credit cards.

I wanted to buy a used digital video camera that was lauded as nearly new. This guy selling the camera, by the name of Charles Allen (beware if you know him, because he's a shyster), didn't take credit cards, and I didn't trust sending him a personal check. Then I remembered those convenience checks. I rushed to my drawer and dug through the credit card applications until I found them. How convenient. I could send the guy a check to pay for the camera, but wait to activate it until I have camera in my possession. That way I wouldn't get ripped off.

I'm no dummy.

So, I called Large Nameless Generic Bank.

My question was clear. "I received these convenience checks that say, 'Call this number to activate these checks!' Does that mean this check isn't good until I activate it?"

"Yes, sir."

"I want to use them to protect myself on a purchase. Can anyone else call this number to activate the check?"

"No, sir."

Thank you and good-bye.

This quick exchange led me to believe that I could sign the check, fill it out, write an amount, but the check still wouldn't be good until I activated it, like some sort of check bomb that would explode into money.

It was a fifteen-second conversation. I didn't get a name, but their names don't matter anyway. Somehow all these individuals morph into one giant collective and evil bank, unless you speak rudely to them, in which case they inform you that they just work for them.

"Well, when you talk to them go ahead and pass on what I just said to you."

Thinking I was protecting myself, I sent Charles Allen a convenience check for $1,200. Well, interestingly enough, as it turns out, all that is needed to activate

Banks are determined to manipulate us in any way possible. This is why their language is purposely vague.

the check is my signature. Something Charles understood because he cashed my check and never sent me the camera. I thought I was protecting myself by using these checks, but all I was doing was exposing my small, small brain.

You may ask, "How stupid can you be?"

Dumb enough to believe a bank.

I'm that dumb.

umers have an average credit card debt of $11,000
thirteen different credit cards.[12]

versal this average dumbness is.

⌐⌐⌐ are determined to manipulate us in any way possible. This
is why their language is purposely vague. President Obama signed the
Plain Writing Act of 2010 to ensure that the language the federal government uses in explaining things to Joe and Jane Public is understand-
able. It passed in the House of Representatives by a vote of 386 to 33.
The 33 who voted against it were lawyers. I assume.

When will they take such action with banks? They keep the rules in
fine print and the explanations vague while urging us to spend more
money. They manipulate our addiction to spending and tease our consumer instincts. When you do try to clarify the meaning of something
with them, even their customer service representatives don't get it. If
they got it, they would have given me a better explanation of how a
convenience check works.

We've been sold a bill of goods.

The problem with credit cards is that they bill us for the goods we've
been sold in the bill of goods that propagates this idea that we need
credit cards. Not only are we continually told that we need credit cards,
but we're told we need them to live a certain kind of life.

World famous film director Martin Scorsese did an American Express commercial where he's picking up photos from his grandson's fifth
birthday party and he's unhappy with the narrative thread of the pictures. It's not perfect. He needs to reshoot; thus he pulls out his American Express card and buys more film. The message is clear: don't hire
Martin Scorsese. He can't even keep his grandson's birthday party under budget.

Yet we still think we need plastic to create a life worth living.

Rich people have money because they have no debt. "Seventy-five
percent of the Forbes 400 (rich people, not your broke brother-in-law
with an opinion) said the best way to build wealth is to become and stay
debt-free."[13]

Look, I don't know what the Forbes 400 is either, but that's probably because I'm not rich. I used credit cards just like you and have nothing to show for it, besides twenty-five pounds in weight gain from fancy restaurants.

"This food is really rich."

"You ain't kidding, baby."

I could buy all those meals with a debit card.

You can do everything with a debit card that you can with a credit card, except pay $4,000 a year in interest fees.

You can rent a car with a debit card, check into a hotel, buy a ceramic kitty online, and pay for midget clowns to entertain at your child's birthday party. Credit cards aren't safer than debit cards. That's a myth. Bullets penetrate credit cards just as easily as debit cards. The truth, is Visa has a zero-liability policy that protects you from all suspicious transactions on their network, both credit and debit.

You can pay for all the same things with a debit card that you can with a credit card. Oh, the only difference is—you have to have money in your bank account. And that's the only reason we use credit cards. Because we got no money. The worst reason in the world to use a credit card.

Today, we paid off six credit cards. That's good news, right? Kind of. Remember? We are the ones handling the accounts. We were one day late on two of them. Right. Paying off debt and we still can't pay on time. So I called them and said, "Hey, if you don't charge us this late fee, we will pay the entire thing off now." Do you feel tempted, Big Bank That Wants Us to Keep Making Payments for the Rest of Our Lives?

They answered, "Good for you. We're still charging you the late fee."

I keep hearing stories about how people call their credit card companies and just ask them to lower their interest rates, and the banks are like, "Sure. Cool." Does that really happen?

So, the good news is that we paid off six accounts.

The bad news is that we paid off six accounts while incurring extra charges.

Banks are not your friends. They are evil witches who live in gingerbread houses, and they will eat you alive. That is their goal. Credit card debt is what a bank uses to capture you and lock you in her cage.

We still have two gigantic cards that triple the debt of these six small ones we just paid off. So we're not out of the woods just yet. So the jubilation is short-lived. I keep thinking about all the money we had in the bank before we paid these bills off. It's a wonderful feeling to have money in the bank. Life feels more secure. Until we "click" six payoffs to these banks. Now that money is gone. Life is back to normal. I can't wait to be out from under the evil spell of these last two cards.

When you pay out to banks by using credit cards, you can't save any money.

If you can't save any money, you stay poor.

Do the math.

Okay, if you're like me, math isn't your strong suit.

If you want to be rich someday, CUT UP YOUR CREDIT CARDS!

You have time now. There's a chapter break.

PART THREE:

MONEY AND YOUR DREAMS

(or You Can't Afford Dreams, So Get Back to Work)

THE GREAT DEPRESSION
(And Other Emotions Associated with Debt)

....

Depression makes you want to give up.

That's why this book is so short.

I was depressed when I wrote it.

Financially related depression is just the opposite of the blanket that makes Harry Potter invisible. With depression, this big, wet blanket covers you, but it's invisible to everyone else. People can still see you, but not the blanket covering you. You feel alone, you and your invisible wet blanket against the world.

You move slower.

You think slower.

Everything slows down, except the phone calls from creditors.

So how do you get through it?

I suggest drugs and alcohol. At least that way you have a great excuse for your financial ruin. People will whisper things like, "That poor guy lost everything because of drugs and alcohol."

Unfortunately, I was sober when I made my poor financial decisions.

I've made my living as a stand-up comedian for more than twenty years now. Whenever I contemplate my career (which I'm always hesitant to call it, because it's more like having friends over, sitting around the living room, and talking to them—except you have a mic), I'm always amazed and thankful that I've been able to support my family. All because of jokes. It's a rewarding feeling.

Most of the time.

These days having a nontraditional career means that the money doesn't traditionally flow into our lives the way it did a year or two ago. With things like scripts and books, you do a lot of work before you get paid, so sometimes the money doesn't flow at all. But if you want to be a writer, there's no other way to go about it.

I want to be a writer.

There's a saying about writing by the author Derrick Jensen: "Writing is really very easy. Tap a vein and bleed onto the page. Everything else is just technical."

They don't want jokes every paragraph, but being humorous now and then wouldn't hurt. No problem, I can add humor like a chef uses spice.

That's if you're fortunate enough to get a book deal. Sometimes the greatest pain comes before you even get the gig. I'm sure you know the feeling. You desperately need money, and along comes a deal, an offer, a proposal, a plan that sounds like it could change your financial situation. So you put everything into it, every fiber of your being and whatever multigrain cereals you can get your hands on. Whatever will help you close this deal. You commit. You go forward, full steam ahead. And . . . and . . .

So while my literary agent is peddling my goods (a book proposal called *Saying Grace with Atheists: Sticking a Fork in Unbelief*), a publishing house likes the tone of my writing, and they want to consider me for a book idea they have about the seven deadly sins, in which overspending is not even mentioned. They want one book per sin. This is very good news (as far as news about sin goes). We have a seven-book deal on the table. I'm delighted at the thought. It would bolster my writing career, and the advance from the deal could get us out of debt. All we have to do now is sit and deliver. (I write in a chair.)

However, the acquisitions editor at the publishing house lets us know that not everyone on the acquisitions team thinks I can pull it off. "He's a comedian. Not a theologian." They don't want a humor book on the seven deadly sins. They want something serious but whimsical in tone. They don't want jokes every paragraph, but being humorous now and then wouldn't hurt. No problem, I can add humor like a chef uses spice. I assume.

Let's get to it.

I research and write and then research and write some more while trying not to dream about how a seven-book deal could establish this writing career I'm really hoping will develop. Plus, the advance on this deal could get us out of debt completely. *Don't think about it.*

So for the next month I research and pound out 20,000 words (four chapters) for the first book in the tentatively titled series *The Seven Deadly Sins (To Name Just a Few)*. I think it's a pretty catchy title. For a book on sin, anyway. In the sample chapters, I cover the story of the seven deadly sins, give a cultural commentary on the sin at hand (pride; for example), expound on the history of pride, and end with a chapter on personal application. (Not how to apply pride to your life but how to overcome it. Living at poverty level is one way, but not recommended.)

Finally, we send the acquisitions editor at the publishing house the sample chapters on pride.

He really likes the tone, gives me a few suggestions, and I go back and rewrite for another couple weeks. This is all on spec, by the way. "Spec" means you don't get paid unless they decide to make a deal. I'm not sure what spec is short for. Speculation? That's probably it. You're gambling on your talent. Anyway, my lit agent sends in the updated material and the acquisitions editor loves it. Says I've hit all the right notes. This is a winner. But we're not done. Now, he has to take it to a team of acquisitions editors who will read it and decide if I get to advance to the next level. It's like a reality show that no one watches except my lit agent and me.

A week later, he calls my lit agent back to let us know that everyone on the team loves it. He says even some of the naysayers who thought I couldn't pull it off are impressed. That's hoop number one. This is going great. My lit agent and I try not to high-five each other. Thankfully, he's one state away so we're spared this embarrassing cultural practice. We know we've got nothing, and yet, this could be everything. I try not to think about the weight of debt being lifted off my shoulders from the advance.

In the back of my mind I suppress the temptation of certain fantasies, like adding up the advance per book, carrying the zeroes and applying them to our newly developed budget, checking off the bills that we could wave good-bye to if this deal comes through. Sure, the thoughts pop in my mind, but I shake my head to erase them with the Etch A Sketch brain God has blessed me with. Still, there are flashes, glimpses in my mind, like of Dinika and me burning our Target Visa. Our little girls laughing in the background. We're standing on the porch of our beloved Victorian house, which we get to keep, by the way, because I've landed this seven-book deal.

I twist my neck from side to side to rid my mind of such thoughts.

Refocus.

The next hoop is the marketing team. The acquisitions editor takes it to them to see if they think seven books is even a good idea. It's takes him a couple of weeks to meet with the head of marketing. The head of marketing says she'll have to read over what I've written.

Tune in next week.

Another week goes by.

The acquisitions guy calls my lit agent and says, "Marketing approved the series. They think seven books on the seven deadly sins will make a bigger splash than one book on the seven deadly sins." We think so too.

Hoop number two is cleared.

The final hoop, he has to take the idea to the board for final approval. The word "board" has us all scared. They don't sound whimsical. They sound "board." We soon learn that the board will not be reading the sample chapters. The acquisitions editor will type a one-page synopsis of everything regarding this book idea and that's what the board will make their decision based upon. This meeting is three weeks away. This is going to be a substantial investment, the acquisitions editor warns. But he's optimistic.

All we have to do now is wait.

Some more.

It's the season finale of our reality show.

In the meantime, I continue to push away all thoughts that lend themselves to fantasizing about making a living as an author or any thoughts about how the advance on a seven-book deal would pull us completely out of debt. One day at a time.

My literary agent calls. It's the climax of the season finale.

"Good morning," he says flatly.

I ask him to hold a second so I can put the earpiece to my phone in, but I can tell from the way he said "good morning" that I should expect bad news.

"What's up?"

"The board said there's nothing funny about the seven deadly sins," he says.

Our instincts were right. They're not whimsical.

"Well, that's because they didn't read my sample chapters," I say.

"They rejected the idea outright."

I've been voted off the island. I don't get a rose. My phone-a-friend doesn't know the answer. Donald fires me. I'm the biggest loser. Or not the biggest loser, because the biggest loser on that show is the biggest winner I think. Whatever.

Anyway, I endure the shock and go about my day.

Until my evening prayer walk.

It is my habit to take a walk around our neighborhood in the evening and pray during the walk. If it's still light out, I slip my iPhone's earpiece in so people don't think I'm nuts, walking around and talking to myself. That's when it hits me. I am devastated. I feel a deep sense of loss. This confuses me, because I didn't spend any time fantasizing about what would happen if they said yes to the deal. When the thoughts came, I pushed them away. Then I realized why it reached so deep. I had spent so much time researching and writing that this book idea became a big part of my life. Now it was gone.

We were going through Philippians. I understood the words. I believed the words. I just couldn't shake this depression.

I thought about my wife's miscarriages.

Before we had our first child, Dinika miscarried twice. It was hard on me but even more devastating to her because she carried the children. I know it's not the same as losing a child, but that's what it felt like. I was pregnant with septuplets. "You're going to have seven books." And then the doctor walks in and tells me they're all dead. Miscarriage. I tried not to get my hopes up, but it's difficult to detach when you invest so much time and energy and whole grain cereal.

Just a week before I had spoken at our church and said, "If you're a Christian, really, what's the worst case scenario for your life? That you lose your home or reputation? That your spouse leaves you? That you're diagnosed with cancer? That someone kills you? If to live is Christ, there is no worst case scenario for a Christian."

We were going through Philippians.

I understood the words.

I believed the words.

I just couldn't shake this depression.

For two days I am completely despondent, unable to pray without weeping over this loss of creative life. I go to my office to work and end up piddling around until noon when I realize I'm not getting anything done. Snap out of it. That's what I tell myself anyway, trying to sound like Cher in *Moonstruck*. I take walks and talk to God about it. "Why are you cast down, O my soul, and why are you in turmoil within me?"[14] Giving myself pep talks: "Ah, you're in debt, and you just lost a book deal that could have got you out. Shake it off. It's only a book deal. God continues to provide for the mortgage each month. You have a lovely, supportive wife who believes in you. Two children whose smiles ignite joy in you. It's only a book deal. A really, really, really good book deal. The heart of every person is in the hands of God. He could have swayed the board in another direction, in a whimsical direction. He did not and that is best."

I know this in my mind, but I am still dejected.

I pray for God to pull me out of this.

He does.

I receive some encouraging news about another project the next day.

I'm not going to tell you what it is because I don't want to get my hopes up.

Halfway through our slow trudge out of debt, it feels much the same. There are setbacks and tiny bits of progress followed by more setbacks, and even after just under a year sometimes it feels like we can't make it. Especially after I receive a call that says the radio station is canceling the show in Nashville. We are counting on that money. Well, we were. It's not there anymore. My wife mentions thoughts of bankruptcy again. I say, "No." Then she says, "I know. God always shows me different." Then I receive a call and book another gig for the month. It looks like we'll make the mortgage after all.

You might be feeling the same way, like something's gotta give. Something will give, but don't let it be you. It may take longer than you anticipate, but don't give up now. Wait for your bit of encouraging news. Don't worry. It's on the way.

I don't feel dejected anymore.

Sure, I still feel this cloud of debt over my head, but at least I can look up.

I know where my help comes from.

10

REAL ESTATE FUN PARK
(The Scariest Ride in the Land)

....

I like to do things around the house. It helps refocus my mind, and it feels productive. This is something I do after I've just completed a project, to reward my wife for her patience with me being holed up somewhere writing (usually Starbucks) for weeks. It's also something I do when I'm depressed, which is when hammers are most useful. When I need to get my mind off things, like the devastating loss of . . . okay, this isn't helping. The point is, I restored much of our historic home myself, putting much of my own blood and sweat into it. Had I been better with a hammer, maybe there wouldn't be so much blood and sweat in our home. I'm not really handy. I'm just cheap and determined. There's a store for cheap and determined people. It's called Home Depot.

Maybe you've seen me at Home Depot. I'm the guy maneuvering a dust-laden cart piled with tools and boards and placards of plywood and cement and tiles and peat moss . . . trying to go through the self-checkout lane. That irksome automated voice keeps telling me, "Please place the item back on the bin."

I scan it again.

"Please place the item back on the bin."

Scan.

"Please, place . . ."

"It's on the bin!"

Folks, if you can't check-it-out-yourself, you probably shouldn't do-it-yourself.

As you will see, both in home restoration and real estate wheeling and dealing, I am a do-it-yourselfer oblivious to the forces shaping me— good old American greed, meaning I am American and greedy, something I didn't know about myself until I started writing about money. Anyway, you should never wheel and deal in real estate, unless you're selling mobile homes.

When we bought our first home in 1998, the mortgage company required a 10 percent down payment, proof that we had $5,000 in savings and 7,000 box tops of our favorite cereal to make sure we were eating the most important meal of the day. Ten years later, when buying our fourth home, the bank required a pen filled with ink, exactly no money down (and no less), and a "stated income." If you aren't familiar with the ultra safeguarded system of the stated income that banks adopted during the housing boom, it went something like this:

"Do you ever get paid?"

"Yeah."

"Sign here."

That's all there was to it.

Thanks, Wall Street!

No one foresaw this would soon entail a mass default of home loans. Well, a couple people foresaw, but no one on Wall Street listened to them. [15]

Wall Street is the center of American finance, the creamy filling of the United States. All those men and women shouting at each other in Oliver Stone films somehow affect whether you and I can buy homes.

Is Wall Street alone to blame for all the front yards of foreclosed homes filled with overgrown plants? No, of course not. A faulty batch of Scott's Weed Killer is probably the culprit. Other than weed killer, maybe the federal government played a part. But does the responsibility finally rest with the government? Not in theory. In theory, we are to blame because the government is "we the people."

Thanks for the adjustable-rate mortgage, neighbor! Democracy is the theory anyway. Oligarchy seems more the reality sometimes. The rich get to make up the rules.

Our story illustrates what happened in America during the Almost-Second Great Depression. During our money meltdown I started thinking about my part in this whole housing debacle, and that included my part as a Christian. I should have left well enough alone. The problem with introspection is that sometimes God lets you see your soul. Talk about *What Not to Wear.* I'll tell you what not to wear—your own righteousness, because you'll find out that it's filthy rags. And other spiritual lessons from reality TV.

The spiritual element to this whole housing mess is not pretty. It's spandex and a bright pink blouse. It's our financial soul.

Then credit card companies, which I once saw as the enemy, seemed loose and friendly. Every week we received some sort of incentive to charge something.

Okay, it's my financial soul. You'll have to search your own soul to find your own bad outfit.

The year was 1998, our first home was listed at $250,000, and just one week after we signed the papers, the price for the same type of home in the same development soared by $25,000. One week later and we wouldn't have been able to qualify for the home we just bought. This was before bankers lost their minds. Suddenly the most frightening experience of our lives turned into this exhilaration that we made the right decision. We went from feeling uncertain to feeling financially wise. Okay, we felt fortunate at first. The self-deception of feeling financially wise would come later when the bankers lost their minds, when the Deceitfulness of Riches called out, "All-in."

Then credit card companies, which I once saw as the enemy, seemed loose and friendly. Every week we received some sort of incentive to charge something, such as convenience checks or a preapproved credit card. An actual credit card, just waiting to have some of that shine rubbed off. All because we were now homeowners.

When we went to pick out cabinets and whatnot for our first new home, people were lined up outside the office of this housing development with lawn chairs and coolers, all waiting their turn to get in on the American Dream. We waltzed past them all because we had been here a week earlier, just ahead of the crowd. Soon we started to believe we actually were real estate geniuses. Four years later that home was worth $450,000. The housing boom made us feel like the blessings would never cease. Real estate was a new ride at Disneyland. The housing boom bamboozled banks, buyers, and busters, the entire country blinded by the big sales event. And it all seemed quite legitimate because there were official papers and math involved. Once upon a time, you had to be rich to live in a half-million dollar home. Now, you just had to be dumb enough. (And I don't mean you in the sense of you, but in the sense of me.)

But did we stay in our first home for four years?

Oh no.

We sold it after two years.

Why?

So we could buy a bigger home, a nicer home with more rooms, higher-end faucets, and a third garage stall to house our cat's litter box, my dream since childhood.

When flipping homes became the fad (these days it's recommended that you flip coins), Dinika and I flipped a home with another couple and came out just by the hair of our chinny-chin-chins, not that my wife or his has a goatee, but just the same.

Our house-flipping business all started with the home of an acquaintance who was in a must-sell situation. I'll call him Bill (because he won't answer to that, and if he ever reads this, I don't want to face him). His story was the same as many people's: his mother-in-law cosigned their home loan with his wife. That's how they ended up in a home that cost them $120,000 in 2001. They refinanced the house twice, so their original $120,000 loan grew to around $200,000. That's what Abominable Credit Monsters do. They grow.

Bill's wife worked but wasn't making enough to keep them out of the red, so the bank gave them the option of losing their home or selling it. They decided to sell. And fast. Bill offered the home to my friend (I'll call him Mr. Chinny-Chin-Chin), and he declined because he didn't know anything about flipping homes. But after Mr. Chinny-Chin-Chin told me about it, I couldn't stop talking about it. "It's real estate! Why let not knowing anything stop us? We could flip that house together and make a killing."

"I don't think we need to kill Bill to flip the home."

"No. Make a killing financially."

"How do you kill money?"

We *really* didn't know anything.

I didn't have an amazing-grace attitude toward the misfortunes of Bill. I blamed his situation on him completely. Whether this was true or not doesn't matter. What matters is that I was willing to take advantage of the misfortune of another without batting an eye or asking many questions about his situation. Our cash flow was stellar. Things were good for us. Things were bad for others. Oh, well. *We're* thankful.

Beware the arrogance that riches can foster.

Later, Mr. Chinny-Chin-Chin and I decided to reconsider Bill's offer but were told that another acquaintance of ours had stepped in and taken him up on it. I'll call him Punch, because that's what he beat us to. The home was no longer available for us to flip.

Punch was in real estate, so Bill trusted him. What Punch didn't tell Bill was that his home was worth a lot more than what Punch had bought it for, which was why Punch made $80,000 after flipping it. That's one side of it. The other side of it was that Bill was in a bad situation and needed to sell right away, a situation I have a lot more sympathy for now that I've experienced a total money meltdown myself.

But at the time we kicked ourselves. Right in the Chinny-Chin-Chin. Yes, we kicked ourselves for not taking advantage of someone else's misfortune. Our capitalism was informing the gospel, rather than the gospel informing our capitalism. We got it backward, blinded by the lure of easy money.

Seeing that Mr. Chinny-Chin-Chin and his wife were renting a home when the market was still booming, I suggested we flip their home since their landlord wanted to sell it. At the time, our credit was stellar, so my wife and I became the primary owners of Mr. Chinny-Chin-Chin's home, and we went to work—fresh paint, new wood floors, sod in the back-yard, and flowers in the front. After paying our day laborers with a Kennedy silver dollar that they could split among themselves and whacking a "for sale" sign in the ground, we were in the real estate business. Now we had two mortgages.

Just as the first payment was due, just as we started getting nervous, just as we considered that we might have made a huge miscalculation and overpaid our day laborers—someone bought the home. We each made about $10,000 on the deal, which disappointed us. I mean, Punch made $80,000. That could have been us! Oh, the deceptive lure of easy money.

We just needed to find the right home to flip, that's all.

So we looked for another home to flip, but noticed the market slip-ping just a bit. That's when we found the next home to flip would be the one we were living in. We paid $300,000 for it and asked $450,000. Someone offered us $25,000 less than what it was listed for, and we were insulted. Don't treat us like that! We wanted to make a killing.

It's not like we needed to sell our home, but the papers kept print-ing articles about people who sold their homes in California and paid cash for homes in other states like Texas, then moved to the Lone Star State and are now stranded there with the Dallas Cowboys. There were reality TV programs about flipping homes. It looked like easy money on TV. Punch made some easy money, so we even had a flesh-and-blood example. The stories just kept coming. We didn't want to leave California. We just wanted in on the Real Estate Fun Park. It was a revival of the 1950s. Then the market dropped a bit more, and the next offer came in at $50,000 less than the asking price. Okay, reality was starting to settle in a little. But very slowly.

After three months, we sold our third home and cleared $100,000, which was $100,000 less than our goal. Our initial plan was to use some of the money to restore the old Victorian home we bought, use some as a down payment, and put some away. This was a good plan. Now, we had some choices to make. Our Christian real estate agent (who's no longer in the real estate business, by the way) counseled us to consider an adjustable-rate mortgage because she assured us that we could refinance our home in three years to a thirty-year fixed. *What's the worry? Prices have leveled off, but they'll come back up.* The blind leading the blind seems too innocent. How about the greedy leading the greedy?

In our case, flipping our home became a financial pattern, and we believed things were okay. We thought this was a normal way to live. I mean, it was a way out of debt. We'd buy a home and within two years acquire enough debt to say, "Well, I guess it's time to sell the house . . . again." Four homes in ten years during the housing boom. Any idiot who held on to his or her money made a killing. Not us. We bought an old Victorian that needed a kitchen restoration.

Wow!

We have a nice kitchen.

The thing that's ironic about this whole fiasco is that the loan we currently have is now impossible to get. You can't get an ARM loan with a stated income these days. Somehow banks didn't see this as a bad idea at the very beginning. But the thing that is most difficult to deal with is neglecting the truth that all of us know: If it sounds too good to be true, there's a real estate agent involved.

My brother-in-law, Paul, the multimillionaire, always gives us good

We took advantage of the loans because they were there. We took advantage of the homes because they were there. We took advantage of the financial misfortunes of others because they were there.

advice. In my gut, I knew before we signed on for this loan that I should call him. He is a savvy business executive. Thus the multi-millionaire thing. I thought of calling him several times, but then my wife and I started talking about how much it would cost to renovate the historic home we wanted to buy. With an adjustable-rate mortgage, we could buy the home for no money down, just like in those commercials, and use the rest to restore the home to its former glory. I hate to say we were fools, but we were fools. Who believes commercials?

We took advantage of the loans because they were there.

We took advantage of the homes because they were there.

We took advantage of the financial misfortunes of others because they were there.

The key to the spiritual underpinnings of all the above is "took advantage," a phrase that used to have negative connotations. Now, it just means that you got while the getting was good.

It's amoral to the hard-core capitalist.

Immoral to people of faith.

Or it should be.

As Christians, where was the gospel to inform our views on these matters? The culture swept us along. We were in the world and of the world. Greedy with entitlement to the American Dream.

It's a shameful thing to call yourself greedy, especially when I didn't see myself as greedy. I preach against the prosperity gospel that teaches people that God wants Christians to be rich. It's blasphemy. It's a different gospel. I preach the truth. And that's why I have to call my sin by name. If it's greed, you call it greed, not a desire for nice things. The temptation is to write all this in the past tense. But the immediacy of present tense makes me feel a healthy shame, which makes me continually ask myself, "Is this the kind of Christian you want to be?"

Once you find your own judgmental self in the same type of situation, which I do, suddenly you have a lot more empathy for others. God doesn't treat us as our sins deserve, but that doesn't mean we might not lose our home. God tells us why He takes our money away from us sometimes. "Why should a fool have money in his hand to buy wisdom when he has no sense?"[16] It's a painful truth because unlike most parents God is not permissive. Like the wise parent that He is, He might allow the consequences of our actions to be our discipline. He doesn't pamper us. He disciplines us so that we may share in His holiness, not the American Dream.

The misfortune of others looks a lot different to me these days.

There but for the grace of God . . . goes my home loan.

11

THE NEW AMERICAN DREAM
(Loan Modification)

....

The website for the California Housing Finance Agency features a slogan: "Keep Your Home." That's a good slogan. So far, so good.

Near the slogan is a photo of a couple standing outside of their home with their arms around each other, their backs to us, looking at their home. Hmmmm. Did they get to keep their home? I can't see their faces. I don't know if they're happy or shooting tears like a squirt gun. If that picture is meant to convey a happy ending, well, it fails. It's ambivalent. They're outside. Are they taking one last look at their home? If the folks at CHFA want to create a feeling of security in potential home losers, they should show a photo of a couple sleeping in bed with smiles on their faces. I can imagine many scenarios for that, and they're all good.

I checked out the website because my mortgage company just told me to call back in fifteen minutes. I guess they're a little busy these days. To kill time, they tell me to check out makinghomesaffordable.com, which is where I see the backs of this couple who may or may not get to keep their home.

After mulling over the site, I call back and listen to the options the robot secretary gives me and then listen to some stale picnic blanket jazz for about five minutes. To avoid dealing with us, maybe their goal is to drive us to suicide. Hence, banal saxophone jazz .

Someone finally answers.

When I tell her I want to talk to someone about a loan modification, she tells me to call the number I just called to reach her. I'm not making this up. "That's the number I just called," I say.

"Let me connect you."

"Okay."

She connects me to the number I just called . . . again.

Call back later, our system is still down.

According to the reliability of their system and the familiarity of the employees with each other's whereabouts, I'm not getting my hopes up.

I give it thirty minutes before I call back.

System's still down. Guess their IT guy didn't show up today. They ask for thirty minutes this time. I graciously give them an extension, hoping they'll get the hint.

My wife and I are now in the position to refinance our home. It's been three years. While waiting in line at Starbucks, I'm told by a random stranger that it's extremely difficult to refinance your home. (Here I thought I was praying quietly under my breath, "Help us refinance our home, Lord." I guess He heard me.) Not at all what our trusty Christian real estate agent told us. She's no brother-in-law. Then someone in line tells me that agents got kickbacks by promoting these ARM loans, which teaches me that you should always pray silently in Starbucks, otherwise these people will be right up in your business.

Refinancing is not something I'm looking forward to, because every story I've heard so far (in line at Starbucks anyway) has included a minimum of 250 phone calls to the mortgage company, dealing with different people each call. I wonder if they'll ask me about how much

I spend at Starbucks. I thank my barista and all the customers for the financial lesson and head back home.

Later, I call back. *Ring, ring.* Robot lady. *Press number 2.* Picnic blanket jazz.

Then a real person answers and asks, "Are you calling about (unintelligible) program for refinancing?"

"I don't know," I say. "I'm calling about whatever programs are available for refinancing."

She informs me in a very slight but unidentifiable accent that the Obama administration has a program to prevent homeowners from becoming home losers. She doesn't use those words, but that's the idea. If this turns out to be true, President Obama will be my all-time favorite president.

> I didn't think I sounded **defensive,** but maybe I did. **Poor lady.** She is probably **battered daily with** angry potential home **losers.**

"Can you answer a series of questions about your financial status?" she asks.

"Yes."

"Can you make this month's payment?"

Darn it.

We just made this month's payment, thanks to God's miracle of two last-minute gigs during the same weekend.

"Yes," I say dejectedly, expecting to be disqualified immediately.

"Would you like me to set up payment now?"

"Ah, we just paid it. Today. This morning."

"Okay," she says, trusting my check's-in-the-mail speech, which just so happens to be true. "Have you experienced a change in income?"

"Yes. I'm self-employed, and with the change in the economy and the implosion of my booking agency, I'm not making as much this year."

"That's okay, sir. Don't worry. I'm here to help you."

I didn't think I sounded defensive, but maybe I did. Poor lady. She is probably battered daily with angry potential home losers.

"One of the requirements you will need to fulfill to qualify for a loan modification is a hardship letter. Can you write a letter?"

"Dear Phone Support Person, yes I can. Sincerely, Thor Ramsey."

She doesn't laugh, so I'll assume she just smiles. It's the comedian's way.

"Do you occupy the property?"

"Yes. Mostly I occupy the couch, but that is on the property."

Then she asks me about our monthly income and if we happen to have $25,000 or more in gold bricks, bonds, savings, or buried treasure in the Virgin Islands.

"I just lost a seven-book deal," I tell her.

"That's okay, sir. I'm here to help you."

I get the feeling she's reading off a script.

Then she says, "You don't understand! I coulda had class. I coulda been a contender. I could've been somebody, instead of a bum, which is what I am."

Yeah, she's definitely reading off a script.

She tells me to go to their website (I want to ask her if that couple gets to keep their home) and fill out a financial analysis form. We have fifteen days to complete it. "Send it in as quickly as possible because it takes us thirty days to respond. Do you have any questions?"

"No," I say, feeling hopeful, assuming everything worked out for that Web couple.

Keep your home.

That's a good slogan.

Two weeks later we receive a short letter saying that they've received our paperwork and will respond in twenty days. That's good news, because the deadline for this book is in more than twenty days, which means I'll be able to finish this chapter. I pray for a happy ending. But however it goes, it will be a happy ending, right? If all things work together for the good of those who love God and are called according to His purposes, then it's all good. It's amazing how cheery you can be once you embrace Reformed theology.

I'll be back in twenty days with the news.

Or sooner.

* * *

I'm back.

We heard back in about a week.

They said they didn't receive all the documents needed, specifically our business profit-and-loss statements for the last three months. The disheartening thing is that I sent them six months of our profit-and-loss statements with all the other paperwork we filled out. So, I re-fax the statements, and tomorrow I'll follow up with a phone call to make sure they receive it all. If they don't receive all the paperwork, they just assume you're good to go. "Never mind about that loan modification, guys. I don't know what I was thinking."

I call them back the next day, and another robot person says, "Thank you for calling. Your call will be answered in less than one minute. Commercial, blah, blah, blah. Please ask your account representative if you may benefit."

Then a human answers. I never get names. If they give names, I don't hear them. It's just something I lose between the transition from robot to human. Anyway, the human says they did receive my profit-and-loss statements. Then she laughs and says, "More like loss statements, bud." I think. That's what I hear in my head anyway. It's probably not on tape, even though our conversation was recorded for quality control.

"Can I help you with anything else?"

"Well, I have to ask . . . do I benefit?"

"I'm sorry?"

"The robot said to ask if I benefit."

"The robot?"

"The human voice without a person attached."

"I'm sorry, sir. I'm not sure I understand."

"That's okay," I say, happy to be misunderstood by a human being. "This conversation won't go in my file, will it?"

"No."

"Thank you then. Hope to hear some good news from you in twenty days."

"I hope so, too."

"Good-bye, Human Person."

* * *

Later that same year . . .

The mortgage company sent us two letters informing us that . . . well, honestly, I'm not sure what they're informing us because the letters were written by lawyers. I think the first letter says that our loan modification has been denied because we're rich enough. Only a lawyer knows.

> **The housing bust is something God has used like a big highlighter across our country—here's the problem, little children. As a country, we've lost our moral common sense.**

Then we receive another letter dated two weeks later that says they modified our loan on a trial basis. I think. It appears we only have to pay half our mortgage payment for three months and then our "situation will be reviewed to determine the best option," such as a short sale. This is California, so people do dress casually. Who knows? Maybe selling shorts can keep us in our home. Our mortgage company seems to think so.

To clarify things I call them, and even the guy I talk to isn't sure about things. He isn't a lawyer. He suggests I just make the partial payments. My wife just sent in a full payment and they applied it to two months. He says this in itself may disqualify us. "Call back Friday to see if you've been disqualified." So the message they seem to be sending is—you're better off if you just stop making your payments. That'll give you a better shot at a loan modification.

I don't want to wait until Friday, so I call back and speak to someone else for further clarification. She says that we're set up for a loan modification on a trial basis. Okay, but what does that mean? A trial basis? Do we get back to them? "Hey, we tried out that paying-less-per-month thing. I think we like it." Is that it? Or is it from their perspective? "Hey, we tried out that receiving less each month. We don't like it."

We'll know in three months if our trial works out. I'd ask you to pray for us, but by the time this is in print, we're either modified or you can look forward to my next book—*The Short Sale (or Bake Sales & Other Ideas to Make Your Mortgage Payment)*.

Regardless, we have to figure out some way to make our mortgage payment.

This is where the morality of the housing bust comes into play. If you do a casual search on Google for "housing bust," you will find one analyst who insists that homeowners have no more obligation to make their payments than banks that walk away from bad investments without moral wobbling, and the next analyst says that each family needs to evaluate their options, with abandonment as last on the list, and on and on with differing opinions and advice. The housing bust is something God has used like a big highlighter across our country—here's the problem, little children. As a country, we've lost our moral common sense.

This shouldn't be news to most Christians.

So the big question becomes, "Why should we feel morally obligated to sacrifice to make payments to a bank that feels no obligation to us?" For the Christian, the answer is plain and simple, if not unnerving: Because however we treat someone else is how we treat God.

Are banks our neighbor?

Should we love our enemies?

The answers are Vacation Bible School 101, which isn't a bad idea.

Maybe everyone involved in the housing bust needs to go back to Vacation Bible School because a little moral common sense goes a long way.

Unlike an adjustable-rate mortgage.

12

THE SOCCER MOM GOSPEL

(Marketing Jesus and the American Dream)

....

When I was a kid, my dad told me we were the working people. Well, that makes sense, because someone has to be poor. Otherwise, who would there be to vote for all the rich people? If not for us poor people, our whole political process would crumble.

Don't get me wrong. We weren't poor poor. We were just Democrats who weren't in show business. We were the poor people movie stars feel guilty about not being anymore. But then credit cards were invented, so we could be poor without anyone noticing.

But my dad wasn't much for appearances. I was all for appearances. I wanted to live the life of Ricky Robertson, a friend from school who lived in the kind of large new home that only rich people in Dakota City, Nebraska, lived in. That's what I wanted. I wanted to live what I couldn't define as a kid in grade school, what most people come to America for, why most Americans are proud to be Americans. I wanted to live the American dream, which in grade school was Ricky Robertson's life.

Even as a Christian I sometimes take the American Dream for granted, like it's the manifest destiny of our nation, like God has ordained our success and the Statue of Liberty was carved by the Holy Spirit Himself. During my money meltdown, I looked at the American Dream more closely because this seems to be the goal that defines not only my life but the life of the American church—"a land in which life should be better and richer and fuller for everyone."[17] Rather than just take it for granted, I looked at the roots of where the idea of this dream came from in my own life. And asked myself some simple questions like, "Could we be living the wrong dream?"

As a kid, I couldn't define it, but I knew it when I saw it. Like most of us, we know the American Dream when we see it, which is why we buy many of the things we do. We see the American Dream in them. In the big homes with expansive lawns and outdoor fireplace grills and white chairs on the lawn celebrating a graduation or marriage or birthday, in the *Better Homes and Gardens* kitchens and yards and holiday place settings, in palm trees on well-manicured streets, in row after row of large Victorian homes, in golf courses and country club memberships and vacations to exotic places and leisure time that produces fond family memories.

The American Dream is expensive.

It's not that these things are evil in and of themselves, but the marketing of this dream as the goal of life ruins many people financially. It subtly misdirects the focus of the church and the Christian life.

But we know it when we see it. And when we see it, we want it.

I saw it in Ricky Robertson's life.

Ricky Robertson's dad owned the Allis-Chalmers dealership in Dakota City, Nebraska, so he had other people doing his work. I don't think Allis-Chalmers sells tractors anymore or if John Deere put them out of that part of their business, but that's what Allis-Chalmers are—they're orange John Deeres. I'm guessing Allis-Chalmers doesn't sell as much as John Deere, because you just see more green tractors than orange ones. Plus, I imagine that in the farming business a guy named John has a better chance of selling tractors to farmers than a guy named Allis.

Ricky and I were classmates and friends, but when we did exchange occasional verbal jabs, as friends do in elementary school, it had to do with class distinction.

"Yeah, well, what's your dad know? He's just a trucker," he would say to me.

"Yeah, well, my dad said your dad was handed everything to him by his dad on a silver platter."

"Yeah, well, at least my family has a silver platter to hand around."

"Yeah, well, my dad's a good dancer."

That always pretty much ended our debates. Whenever I brought up the dancing argument, he'd just give me a funny look. Yeah, apparently, Ricky's dad couldn't dance worth a hoot. So, what could he say?

Ricky Robertson, along with his dad and mom and older sister, lived in a brand-new split-level (all the rage at the time) home. Me and my dad danced around in an old farmhouse hauled into town years earlier by a semitruck. Even though our home was in "town," the streets surrounding our home were dirt.

> **My contention is that marketing the American Dream in the evangelical church has shaped our view of Jesus.**

I decided at an early age that I didn't want to be a trucker.

My father's American dream was not the one I wanted.

It wasn't just that Ricky lived in a large split-level home, but his parents were college educated. His mother was a teacher who made him tuck in his shirts. His father was involved in the community in a way that my dad was not, like riding Shriner's go-carts in local parades and playing golf at the country club. If my dad used a golf club, it would be to smack the hogs so they'd move into the truck trailer faster.

It wasn't just the house. It was the idea he was living—better, richer, fuller. It's the idea that our country is founded upon—life, liberty, and the pursuit of happiness. It's what makes teenagers long to leave their small, quaint towns for the big city in search of better, richer, fuller lives.

•

It's why preachers can preach messages that promote this idea of "better, richer, fuller," and we don't question it. Didn't Jesus say, "I came that they may have life and have it abundantly"?[18] It's the reason that many believe that God's main concern is our happiness. How many parents have stated, "I just want my children to be happy"? Happiness is the purpose of life in America. It's our underlying philosophy. It's why we're here. Isn't it? It's why the most untrue statement in American Christianity can be uttered without anyone questioning it. It's the anthem of the Soccer Mom gospel: God accepts you just the way you are.

When we focus on one aspect of who Jesus is and neglect the other facets of His character, we end up with a reduced Jesus.

I'm only singling out the soccer moms because they are a specific demographic group that is marketed to in American evangelicalism. My contention is that marketing the American Dream in the evangelical church has shaped our view of Jesus. We have a Jesus who has been developed by marketing, and it affects how we see Christ. Just like our parents, we believe that God's only concerned about our happiness, that He accepts us just the way we are. Far be it for me to burst your soccer mom ball, but God doesn't love us just the way we are. He loves us in spite of the way we are. There's a big difference. If God accepts us just the way we are, then there was no reason for Christ to come to earth and die on the cross. God accepts Christ, and if we are found in Him, God accepts us in Christ. Simple biblical points that can be lost in the American Dream– version of our faith. In one view, Christ is the center. In the other, we are the center. Distinctions that seem subtle but are actually huge.

The Soccer Mom gospel is so prevalent because it's what many of us want to believe. It's the most comforting. It's also popular because we let culture dictate what aspects of Jesus we communicate. When we focus on one aspect of who Jesus is and neglect the other facets of His character, we end up with a reduced Jesus. We don't have the fullness of

Christ in view. "Consider the kindness and severity of your God."[19]

That's why the Soccer Mom gospel sells well on a pillow, a plaque, or a coffee cup. It's marketable. And marketing is all about money. It's okay to fib in church as long as you call it marketing.

Marketing Jesus started during the Victorian era. Religious postcards were very popular during this period, and they depicted a Jesus who was fit for ladies and gentlemen. He was palatable to the prim and proper etiquette-loving Victorians, a gentle Jesus, meek and mild, with long hair and flowing gowns. But their most popular Jesus was the postcard of the helpless little baby Jesus.[20] Just like Ricky Bobby. In the movie *Talladega Nights,*[21] Ricky Bobby also loves the baby Jesus, but his wife objects, telling him that baby Jesus grew up.

But Ricky won't have it and scolds her. "Look, I like the baby Jesus the best. When you say grace, you can say it to grown-up Jesus or teenage Jesus or bearded Jesus or whoever you want."

Then everyone at the dinner table begins chattering about their favorite Jesus.

His racing buddy: "I like to picture Jesus in a tuxedo T-shirt because it says like I wanna be formal, but I'm here to party, too."

Then one of his sons: "I like to picture Jesus as a ninja fightin' off evil samurai."

"I like to think of Jesus with, like, giant eagle's wings, singing lead vocals for Lynyrd Skynyrd with, like, an angel band."

This scene is really an indictment about how we minimize Jesus to suit our own preferences. Sure, it's that accidentally, but it is that.

Even today, one of the most popular versions of Jesus during Christmas season is the little baby Jesus in the manger. That's rooted in our Victorian heritage. That's why our manger scenes are so clean and tidy and sanitary. It's not that it's biblical. It's residual from the Victorian postcards.

David Platt writes of this in his book *Radical,* saying that we are tempted to remake Jesus as "a Jesus who doesn't mind materialism and who would never call us to give away everything we have. . . . A Jesus who is fine with nominal devotion that does not infringe on our comforts, because, after all, he loves us just the way we are. . . . A Jesus who brings us comfort and prosperity as we live out our Christian spin on the American dream."[22]

We customize Jesus to fit our dreams.

It wasn't until years later that I realized something about coveting Ricky Robertson's life: dreams are costly.

I hadn't seen Ricky in years, but I caught up with him at our class reunion this summer. He's a devoted family man now and a Christian, which is always good news to discover. During our brief time together, I asked him how his mom and dad were doing. His brief statement said a lot about how much the American Dream can cost us. "My parents split up. That's why my family is my main priority. I don't want to lose them for those other things."

There was no need for him to define the other things.

We understood.

PART FOUR:

MONEY AND YOUR HABITS

(or Do What Your Money Says: Trust God)

13

IF YOU WANT TO KNOW WHAT GOD THINKS OF MONEY

(Just Look at Who He Gives It To)

....

When I first started flying around the country to perform comedy, I resentfully plodded past the people seated in first class, thinking they were all arrogant snobs. Then I became a frequent flyer, and the airlines started bumping me up to first class as a courtesy. That's when I discovered—I was right.

Now I sit in first class feeling superior as I watch these obviously inexperienced travelers trudge by with their pillows from home and suitcases packed with a month's supply of clothing for their three-day weekend. Money leads to privilege, and privilege leads to warm towels and real silverware in first class. Suddenly we think we deserve all the amenities. We expect the pampering, the namby-pambering of beverages before takeoff, the sleep masks and support pillows with memory foam.

It is nice typing this with the extra elbow room, though.

Oh, I have to put my laptop away for now. My filet mignon is here.

I thought I had right ideas about money. That it won't buy happiness,

Money can produce in us a blinding pride, puffing us up to think more highly of ourselves and our keyless ignition systems than we should.

all that stuff your grandma tells you. Unless she's rich. Even then, she might say it, but we won't believe it. Why? Because she's rich. Money may not buy happiness, but it can make you thankful you're not poor. Most of us think that rich is better. This leads us to think that rich people are better. This leads us to look down on poor people. Especially if we have balconies and they're trimming our hedges. Now, if a Masai herdsman of East Africa told us that money doesn't buy happiness, we might listen.

Might.

Most likely we'd dismiss what he has to say because he's not rich.

He doesn't fly first class.

This won't do. We need to get a grasp on what God thinks of money, especially those He gives it too—the rich. What does God think of rich people? Does He like them less than poor people? Does He want to make us rich? Why aren't you rich? Let's look at these questions that my mother-in-law asks me regularly.

Money often tempts us to feel superior to those with less of it. (That's what my servants tell me anyway.) In this way, money can lead us astray. It can produce in us a blinding pride, puffing us up to think more highly of ourselves and our keyless ignition systems than we should. We should never give preference to the rich over the poor. We're not banks.

Believe it or not, there's even snobbery among those in first class. I am annoyed by the business executives who weasel to the front of the line so they can be the first of the first class to board, thereby securing the precious overhead space they desire. Then my annoyance turns into competition. I stick my leg out or block their passing with my carry-on bag. At first I do it to let the women with children and those who need extra time ahead of the weasels. But then it becomes a fight for that precious overhead space. Soon I am engulfed in the entitlement fighting-to-get-ahead mentality at boarding time.

Even when I recognize the behavior and confess it, shaking my head at myself and saying, "What are you doing? You're a Christian," I have trouble the next flight with the same attitude. It becomes a vicious cycle: fight for spot, confess behavior, then calm down and find some elderly passenger who needs help lifting her carry-on bag into the overhead bin. Not that I don't check her out good, to make sure she isn't a businesswoman posing as a needy senior citizen to get a better spot in line. The greatest misconception about flying first class is that the people in first class are rich people. They just appear that way because they get privileges. All first class really means is that you fly a lot. You can fly a lot to jobs that don't pay much. Most of us want to appear rich or at least richer than we really are. That's one reason we hide our bank accounts like less honorable body parts. Whereas truly rich people don't want to make it obvious that they're rich because then people might ask them for money.

You might be asking, "How can I pretend to be rich?" It's simple. Borrow money. Money is what gives people the impression you're rich, but since people can't see our bank statements, we have to display our riches by buying things. Borrow money to get things, and you too can pretend to be rich. Like Solomon said, "One person pretends to be rich, yet has nothing; another pretends to be poor, yet has great wealth."[23] Don't pretend to be rich (unless you're dating).

By now you understand that I'm not rich. I make a good living, but don't consider myself rich. I'm not poor. At least I don't feel poor. That is, until I'm around my relatives. I have an overachieving bunch of ultra-successful in-laws. One brother-in-law is a three-time Grammy winner who's working on his fourth or fifth (I can't keep up) big band jazz album, and he scores movies that you've heard of, such as *Remember the Titans* and *The Incredibles* to name just two. My other brother-in-law, Paul, the one who designed some kind of computer chip, started a company in Silicon Valley and sold it for half of the city of San Francisco, you've already met.

Oh yeah, and I tell jokes.

I'm always depressed after holiday dinners. Both these guys live in million-dollar homes, and on Thanksgiving Day I have to crawl through the passenger door to start the car because the driver's side handle is broken. Of course, this is California, so a million-dollar home just means you have three bedrooms.

> **Whatever you have, God has provided it for you to enjoy—not that He doesn't want you to share with me. But would you be just as content if He took it all away?**

The thing is, my relatives are well put-together people. They're likable and talented and funny people who just happen to be wildly successful. It's not that I resent my relatives for being rich. I just feel inferior to them, which is much healthier than resentment.

Sometimes we get the idea that all rich and successful people are likable and talented and smart like my relatives. Money doesn't always follow such things. Just look at me. I'm . . . okay, not the most objective case to make, but there are plenty of despondent debutantes and self-destructive rock stars to keep the Lifetime Movie Network happy. The point is, we sometimes have the notion that the rich are more deserving of riches because of the qualities they possess. Rich people aren't superior to poor people. (It only seems that way because we work for them.) Do you really need examples of rich people who aren't smart and talented? Turn on the TV. It's proof positive that the industry overpays untalented go-getters. Money simply fools people into thinking they're as smart and talented as their paychecks. This is the La-Z-Boy recliner common sense of the middle-class at its most basic. Who doesn't know this? Yet, we can still find ourselves believing that rich people are superior to poor people. Why do we attribute great talent to anyone who has great riches? Is it because we live in a celebrity-driven culture?

King Solomon, himself an extremely rich man, wrote of the rich: "Again I saw that under the sun the race is not to the swift, nor the battle to the strong, nor bread to the wise, nor riches to the intelligent, nor favor to those with knowledge, but time and chance happen to them all."[24]

The key point here is "nor riches to the intelligent." Rich people aren't any smarter than poor people. It's just a little something I like to repeat to myself while paying the bills. Some rich people had nothing to do with their wealth. Think of anyone you know who married someone else who has money. Some of them had nothing to do with creating wealth besides picking out the right outfit. Some people just happen to be rich through no fault of their own. Others were industrious and innovative and created wealth through their ideas, imagination, and grit.

But enough about my relatives.

Biblically, riches are not a sign of superior intelligence or of superior spirituality. With that in mind, the apostle Paul makes it clear that it's not wrong to be rich either. He just admonishes the rich to depend "on God, who richly provides us with everything to enjoy."[25] Whatever you have, God has provided it for you to enjoy—not that He doesn't want you to share with me. But would you be just as content if He took it all away? That's a tough question for a rich person to face. If you'd like to know the answer, I'll take a check.

For the most part, churches have strayed into two extremes about money. Some Christians believe material blessings mean the favor of God on a person's life. They take some wonderful verses about God's provision for His people—"beloved, I pray that you may prosper in all things"[26]—and warp it to mean that all Christians have the right to riches and health, and that the rich are the spiritually superior anointed ones. That's only biblically accurate in Houston, Texas.

Christians in previous centuries emphasized the opposite false doctrine—that you must be poor to be spiritual or that God has called us all to poverty or to shop at Wal-Mart, which, if not a vow of poverty, is at least an acknowledgment of thrift. (Maybe there are some positives to Wal-Mart after all. I hope so, because that's where we shop now.) This goes back to medieval Christians who took the story of the rich young ruler and made it the standard for all believers. They taught that all Christians must give away everything they own and follow Jesus and store up treasure in heaven, the one account you can't access online.

This misses the point of the story. This moral young leader had made money an idol, and that's what Jesus was admonishing. Jesus always puts His finger on the very thing that we idolize, and this varies from person to person. Some idolize money, some prestige, some themselves. We shouldn't idolize money. That's what rock stars are for.

In a rich society it's easy to unknowingly make an idol out of money.

Dinika and I never felt like money was an idol in our lives because we could always point to others who were richer, usually at Thanksgiving dinner. I've come to believe the mark of materialism is that we compare ourselves to people who have more. This way, we are the ones deprived. This way, even rich people can feel deprived.

If you had accused us of being materialistic, we would have denied it and even believed our denial. Our friends would have come forward as character witnesses. That is, unless they wanted to implicate themselves. We don't live lavishly, even though our kitchen could be featured in *Better Homes and Gardens* magazine. We live comfortably. And that's the key. Riches aren't wrong. It's just they can lead to comfortable, complacent lives, not that a *Homes and Gardens* shoot isn't stressful. They can lead us to believe that the dissatisfaction we feel has to do with not having enough. Oh, the deprived rich. If only we had more, then we'd be happy.

When the economy slowed down, so did work.

I am flying less these days, so my frequent flyer status is dropping.

On my connecting flight, I have to fly coach. First class boards first. They all pass me by. Afterward, I board, but the flight attendant asks me to wait at the entrance of the plane so she can pass out a couple of drinks to those in first class. I stand there until she gives me the go-ahead. Then I walk by my usual seat and smile at some elderly woman who's reading the business section of the *Wall Street Journal*. Of course I'm suspicious.

I take my seat in coach with relief and satisfaction.

It feels good to live without delusion.

14

SAVING MONEY SO YOU
CAN GIVE IT AWAY
(The Get to Give to Get to Give Plan)

....

Congratulations! You've made it to the part of Dave's plan that's the most fun: not spending money. Here's what I've come to understand: debt prevents and savings provides. And just for good measure, I'm going to do this: use one more colon.

Depending on which way you lean between those two, you'll feel the weight of it in your daily life. Debt keeps you from doing things and having things, whereas savings provides you with security for tomorrow and the wherewithal to be generous. So get out of debt now. If you're not out of debt, go back to chapter 1, and I'll meet you back here when you're debt free.

Last week we made a final click online, sending a $7,500 check to pay off a final credit card balance. It was a great feeling, even though there was no celebration music. I felt very encouraged about our financial situation. So much so that I spent 99 cents on a song from iTunes, played it for my wife and spun her around in front of the dryer. Then I thought about last month, how much we took in, how many debts we paid off. It filled me with even more determination to stay out of debt because I also thought about how much we could have saved if not for all the debt. For example, we could have saved $7,500. That's something we paid in addition to necessities like Starbucks and the mortgage. Think of it. Saving several thousand dollars a month! That's the new plan. Instead of paying several thousand dollars a month to credit card companies, we save it.

That's the thing about money.

Rich people have more of it.

This reality doesn't seem to change.

Since they have money, they talk about what to do with it, like mutual funds and mid cap funds and the S&P Index and emerging markets and other things that people like me, with no money, have no idea what they're talking about when they refer to their hedgehog. Is a mutual fund a fund my wife and I have in common? I assume. Mid cap, some sort of investment in ball caps, not a large investment, not a small investment, but a mid-investment. It's just right. S&P Index could be anything. Shooting & Pistols Index. Socks & Pajamas Index. Sorry & Pardon's Index, the index used to measure scandals of political figures.

Before we even worry about what investments to make, we need to get one thing really, really, really, really, really, really[100,000]* clear: your income is the thing that will build your wealth.

How?

By saving it.

Then once you save it, that's right, you give it away. Okay, you give some of it away. It's the get to give to get to give plan. As long as we keep it rolling out, God will keep it rolling in, pressed down, shaken and stirred, clean and pressed. How's that go? Let me look it up. Here it is: "Give, and it will be given to you. A good measure, pressed down, shaken together and running over, will be poured into your lap."[27] I'm not talking about a prosperity doctrine that encourages materialism.

* to the [100,000] means that many more times

I'm talking about the doctrine of a generous heart, the cheerful giver policy, because God is a cheerful giver. Sometimes He gives double rainbows and makes hippies cry.

So, how much should we give?

We'll get to that.

First, let's talk about saving some.

When it comes to saving money, the only thing my wife and I have going for us is a life insurance policy that my mother set up that names me as the beneficiary. When she dies, I get some money. And she gets the cheapest funeral possible. Don't worry. My mother and I have discussed this, and it's really what she wants. She doesn't believe in wasting money on something you'll only use once, like a casket.

My wife had a 401k through the company she worked for, but that has since liquidated. So, thanks to my mother, that life insurance policy is it, which is not a strategy most financial counselors encourage—waiting for someone to die. Using life insurance policies as a means of savings can make you root for someone's death, and if they get wind of this while they're alive, they can still change the name of the beneficiary. (Don't worry, sis, your secret's safe with me.)

Many marriages struggle with this issue—one spouse wants to save and one spouse wants to spend.

Saving money is something my wife and I have never agreed on. In our early marriage we maintained separate checking accounts, splitting all the costs like we were roommates. At the time, my wife made way more than I did, so I suggested we save my income and live off hers. She didn't like the idea, and I didn't humbly lead. I just mildly suggested it as a codependent. Part of the reason I was quiet was the separateness of our accounts. And part of the reason was that she made way more than I did. We were not yet living as one flesh. We weren't even living as one checkbook. Living as one flesh doesn't mean you have to use each other's toothbrush, something my wife cannot stomach to this day. It just means that if you're not of one mind on this topic, then you're not going to be saving any money.

The other part of our problem was that I was not leading our home spiritually. Well, I thought I was, but have come to realize years later that I was not. Had I actually been leading our home, I would have led my wife down to the bank and opened a savings account.

Many marriages struggle with this issue—one spouse wants to save and one spouse wants to spend. In my marriage, I'm content to spend the day at home, read a book, take a nap, whatever. But my wife is the opposite. "Come on, let's get out of here," she'll say.

"Why?"

"Let's go do something fun."

"We're doing something fun right now."

"What are we doing?"

"We're saving money. Isn't this fun?"

Saving money is fun.

Do the math.

One way to save money is by having a simple rule of paying yourself first. It's a basic plan taught by many financial experts. When you get paid, you put 10 percent in savings, you give 10 percent to church, and you use the rest to live on. You pay yourself first by putting money into savings. Be careful though, because I've fallen behind in paying myself, and now I'm in debt with myself for $100,000. Unfortunately, I've turned myself over to a collection agency, but they can't seem to get hold of me.

Just make sure you get the order right.

Giving to God first should be our priority, like the Levitical example of "firstfruits" to celebrate the harvest God has given.[28] Then put 10 percent in savings. Now, you can go on living.

Getting out of debt was just the goal to get us to here, the place where we can begin to build our financial portfolio (as soon as we find out what a portfolio is). But this is not about hoarding. This is about saving to provide for the future. However, to save for the future, you have to stay alive.

Out of town, I heard my phone chime around two a.m. that I had a text. It was from my wife: "Pray. Heartbeat is not right."

Dinika was born with a heart murmur, and during the birth of our first child, the OB-GYN said, "It was the first time in my career that I feared for the life of the mother."

I said to him, "I wasn't that mad at her. She couldn't help having our baby during Monday Night Football."

He thought he was going to lose her. Since the birth of our first child, she has been on heart medication. Naturally, her text concerned me. I prayed and texted her back. "Praying for you now."

Then she texted back: "I'm scared." So I texted: "I'm calling you," because I didn't want the ring to scare her to death. That would be bad.

She didn't sound good on the phone.

"Go to the emergency room," I said.

"I can't. We don't have health insurance."

"What?"

> The other aspect of **building wealth** is so you'll have **money** to give away. John Wesley once said, **"Earn as much** as you can and **give away as much as you can."**

"Honey," she explained, "we haven't had health insurance for the last year. It was seven hundred dollars a month."

I guess we hadn't been talking about financial matters as much as we should. That's the thing about nearing the end of your goals. Even this close to the end, you'll find small setbacks. Now that things are looking up financially for us, we have to get this health care business squared away. Otherwise we won't be leaving our children an inheritance, because my wife has no life insurance policy either. If I die, they're covered. If she dies . . . I can't even think about it. I couldn't afford to bury her right now. We've never even discussed the possibility of her dying. I don't even know what her wishes would be. I can't imagine she wants to be buried out back by the cat. But that would be our only option at this point.

I don't know much about insurance, but this is the first time in my life I've even considered sitting down with an insurance salesman, pushing *Death of a Salesman* out of my thoughts because that's my image of spending an evening with an insurance salesperson—like an evening with Death. "We all hate insurance, until we need it," is what Dave Ramsey says.

You see why getting out of debt and staying out of debt is so vital? My wife has been neglecting her health to avoid a seven-hundred-dollar-a-month health insurance payment because we weren't money enough ahead to pay it. Being in debt could cost you your life. That's just one reason building wealth is important. For the sake of your family's security.

The other aspect of building wealth is so you'll have money to give away. John Wesley once said, "Earn as much as you can and give away as much as you can." That's a memorable quote because that's the proper Christian view of money. As God generously provides, we generously give. Or maybe as we generously give, God generously provides. Clearly, the Bible teaches Christians to be generous, and it also teaches that God will take care of us. That's why we don't have to fear being generous.

What I did have to fear is my wife making it through the night.

I prayed for her over the phone, and she told me she was going to try to get some sleep. "I'm leaving at four-thirty this morning," I said, "so let me know how you are if you're up."

Then I tried to sleep.

I received another text at 4:21 a.m. from my wife: "Okay right now to sleep." I texted back: "Keep me updated. I don't wanna lose you." Who would find all the stuff I misplace?

My ride dropped me off at the Oakland airport. Just after checking in, my wife texted me: "I'm hoping Daniel can listen to it today and tell me something. It is beating so weird." Daniel is a member of our church who is doing his residency as a budding young doctor. He has a stethoscope in his car, which comes in handy whenever my wife is about to die.

I texted her: "Have you not been asleep yet?"

"I slept an hour. When I picked Kate up from crying, it got worse."

"Call me."

She sounded worse and couldn't talk for long.

It was Sunday, the day we normally struggle with tithing, not health issues. It seems things like this always come into play when we consider how much to tithe. "Well, we have this new doctor bill and that expense and whatnot and so forth." It always becomes an issue: "How much do we give away, especially when times are tough?"

The greatest temptation of Christians in financial trouble is to hold back giving. Well, that's not completely accurate. The greatest temptation of Christians in America is to hold back giving. The average evangelical Christians in America give only 2 percent of their income to the church. In my own life, I've found that if I don't write that tithe check as soon as I get paid, it may not get written, not because of intentions but because when two people handle the same banking account, suddenly that 10 percent is not there the next week. Sometimes our intention is to tithe, but we delay one week and it's been eaten up by other things, especially if you're living from paycheck to paycheck and discover your wife might have to go to the hospital. Suddenly, our tithe is being reallocated to pay for a trip to urgent care, which she texted me "opens at 7 a.m."

> **Many of us are surprised when we get to the end of the year and discover how little we've given to the church.**

I texted her: "Go. I'm boarding. Talk to you when I land. Love you!"

When it comes to tithing, it's always something.

This is why so many of us are surprised when we get to the end of the year and discover how little we've given to the church. We had no idea we fell in that 5-percent-and-under category. We felt like we were being generous. Many times we want to give, but we are so poorly organized that it becomes, "Hey, did we tithe on this check already?"

"I dunno. I think so."

Yeah, we better not give again. That might be too much.

How much is too much?

The standard biblical tithe is 10 percent, but Zacchaeus gave 50 percent of his income.[29] He gave as much as he wanted to, which is really the New Testament standard of giving—give as much as you want. I know that's not practical enough for some of you, so let's define it a little further: How much you got? Okay, let me rephrase that: How big is your heart? Our giving will be in direct correlation to our relationship with Christ, bursting out of the X-ray screen just like the Grinch's. Let's hope that's all that's wrong with my wife. "I'm having chest pains, Doctor."

"Well, according to your X-rays . . . you're overly generous."

The point is, we don't give out of guilt or compulsion or duty or because we're going to get rich in return, but we give out of gratitude because salvation has come to us just like Zacchaeus. We don't give because there's a giving rule like, "No more than all and no less than 50 percent." But if you need a rule of thumb . . . no more than all and no less than 50 percent. *Will the ushers come forward, please?*

The New Testament rule is give generously and cheerfully. This isn't to say the Levitical 10 percent standard should be thrown out the window. It's still a great guideline. The gospel doesn't have to require us to give a certain amount, because if we truly get the gospel, we will give out of gratitude for what God has done. God has given us something much more valuable than a tenfold return on our money. He has given us life. Try to out-give God for that.

So, *how* much should we give?

It's not the question Jesus would ask. Jesus would ask, "How much should you keep?" That's the principle I'm going with here: Save as much as you can, give as much as you can. As average Americans we spend ten times more just on the interest of our debts than we do on giving. This means we could all stand to give a lot more, but sometimes we're afraid to give because of situations we find ourselves in. Proverbs 11:24 (ESV) says, "One gives freely, yet grows all the richer; another withholds what he should give, and only suffers want." You want to get out of debt, give your way out. Seek to maximize your generosity.

So, how much you got?

One moment I'm encouraged by our financial situation; the next I'm worried. This health insurance issue is exactly the kind of thing that can keep us from giving. "How much was your doctor bill?" I don't know yet, and that's where the temptation to hold back comes in. Maybe you're maxed out on debt and feel like you have nothing to give, that it would be irresponsible to give at this point. Oh, *now* we want to get responsible with our money! When there's giving involved.

Situations like this are not uncommon. We neglected to tithe before for one reason or another. And every reason feels like this present one, like a crisis. After we missed tithing one week, the next week I received a call from someone who was producing a show at a comedy club in Hollywood. When they called me for the gig, they stressed it was a fund-raiser for a worthy cause, like a water supply for kids somewhere. After I told them what my standard honorarium was, I said, "But I'll leave it up to you what you decide to pay me, since it's just in LA." Now, I wasn't expecting anywhere near my standard honorarium, but my thinking was that I would take this check (which I assumed would be about 10 percent of what I normally get) and use it for our Sunday tithe. You know? A makeup tithe. After the show, I opened the little thank-you envelope they gave me to behold a $5 Starbucks gift card. That was the first time I've ever been disappointed by Starbucks in my life.

It was disappointing and depressing to not give that Sunday.

Always send a contract, no matter what. It clarifies things, like you expect to be paid in American dollars rather than coffee beans.

Withholding because we're in financial trouble is something we've all probably done. Sometimes we withhold for other reasons. Some of us resent giving, but if we resent giving money to the church, then we need to ask ourselves some questions, like, "Would sermons during Christmas season be less boring without heat?" Or do you have twenty hours during the week to prepare a sermon?

If we resent giving money on Sundays, then we really do have a heart problem. It's quite common, though, for several reasons. We live in a society where we don't have to trust God for daily bread, let alone for any physical ailments. Well, unless you don't have any health insurance. Then you tend to call out to God rather loudly. But for the most part we don't have to trust God for daily needs. We have grocery stores and doctors and dentists, a slew of professionals who look out for our well-being, not that the bagger at Piggly Wiggly is making a career of it. We can be thankful for these things to God, but that's not the same as really trusting God for a life necessity. Even emotional problems are reserved for professional counselors. What do we really trust God for on a daily basis? It's not that we don't believe in God, it's that we don't rely on God. Most of the time, we just don't have to. That's why a financial crisis can really help your faith grow.

Not to mention being without health insurance.

Later, Dinika still didn't feel well, so she went to urgent care. There was no cardiologist available, so the guy at urgent care wanted to call an ambulance and send her to the hospital. You know, so they wouldn't get sued. Dinika asked the guy what he was basing all this on, and his only answer was the heart murmur she's had since childhood. "That's it?" she said to him. "No, I can't go with that. I'll go see my own cardiologist tomorrow. I'm not paying to have an ambulance take me to the hospital where we'll have to pay for staying there, not to mention all the tests." And with that, she handed him the complimentary paper dress and left.

"How do you feel now?" I asked

"I chewed up an aspirin. My heart feels normal now."

This is one gutsy lady. True grit.

I was both thankful and appalled. Thankful that she didn't go to the hospital for the night and appalled that she didn't go to the hospital for the night. But that was our situation. She said to the urgent care guy, "This could break our family financially." So, she took an aspirin. They're cheaper.

Insurance is a lot more important than most of us care to admit.

I never imagined that whether or not we had health insurance would ever play a part in our tithing.

When my wife and I decided to get out of debt, we both determined that we would give the standard 10 percent tithe of every check. Sometimes, before I write that tithe check, I experience an inner spiritual battle. On days like that day at urgent care, that's when I have to remind myself of certain biblical truths, such as, "He who did not spare his own Son, but gave him up for us all—how will he not also, along with him, graciously give us all things?"[30] I remind myself that the promise is for "all things," including my family's well-being, that I can give freely and not withhold. God will take care of us and our necessities. If we need heat, He'll provide heat. If we need health insurance, He'll provide for it. If we need a grande light mocha frappuccino, well, we're on our own.

So I write the check and pray, thanking God that He is good to us and will take care of us. I don't usually write it during the church service, because I don't carry a checkbook around with me.

I'm no dummy.

I write it at home, where I can always change my mind.

15

SLACKER BE THY NAME
(The Recline of the Protestant Work Ethic)

....

N ow I hope you realize that the thing that will build the wealth for you to be generous is your income. In other words, work builds wealth. Not fancy investment tricks. Just plain old hard work. That's right. Work is the preferred method of building wealth, as lottery tickets have proven unreliable and full of false hope. You buy a handful and start scraping away. "My life's gonna be great—"SCRAPE, SCRAPE"—if poor equals great."

"We're gonna take a cruise—"SCRAPE, SCRAPE"—around the block, in the car."

"I'm gonna throw a big party—"SCRAPE, SCRAPE"—for all my invisible friends."

Things like the lottery are subtle because you don't lose all your money at once. Now that would make the lottery exciting, if there was some actual risk involved when you played. You scratch away, and it says, "You owe $10,000." Now that would be losing the lottery. Besides, most lottery winners live out Solomon's proverb: "Wealth gained hastily will dwindle, but whoever gathers little by little will increase it."[31] There are two great tragedies in life: winning the lottery and not winning the lottery.

Counting on something like the lottery is a lazy way to get out of debt.

Work is the best method of building wealth. Its greatest threat is laziness.

I've given this whole lazy thing some thought because my line of work lends itself to slacking off, as do most careers of the self-employed. If you're your own boss, how much trouble can you get in if you call in sick? I've thought about slackers diligently while sitting at Starbucks, doodling on napkins. Consequently, I've doodled so many thoughts about slackers that it really amounts to a short bonus book inside the book you're reading now. How often do you get that? And you thought only DVDs came with extras.

Here are my observations about slackers everywhere, via napkin doodles.

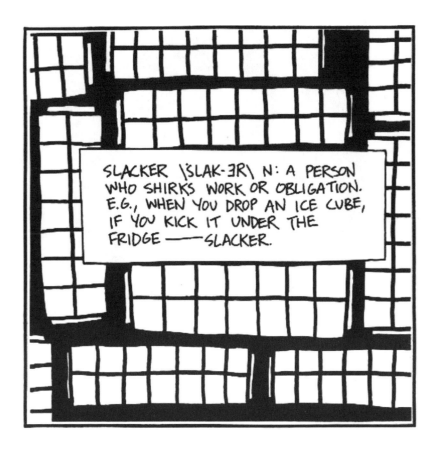

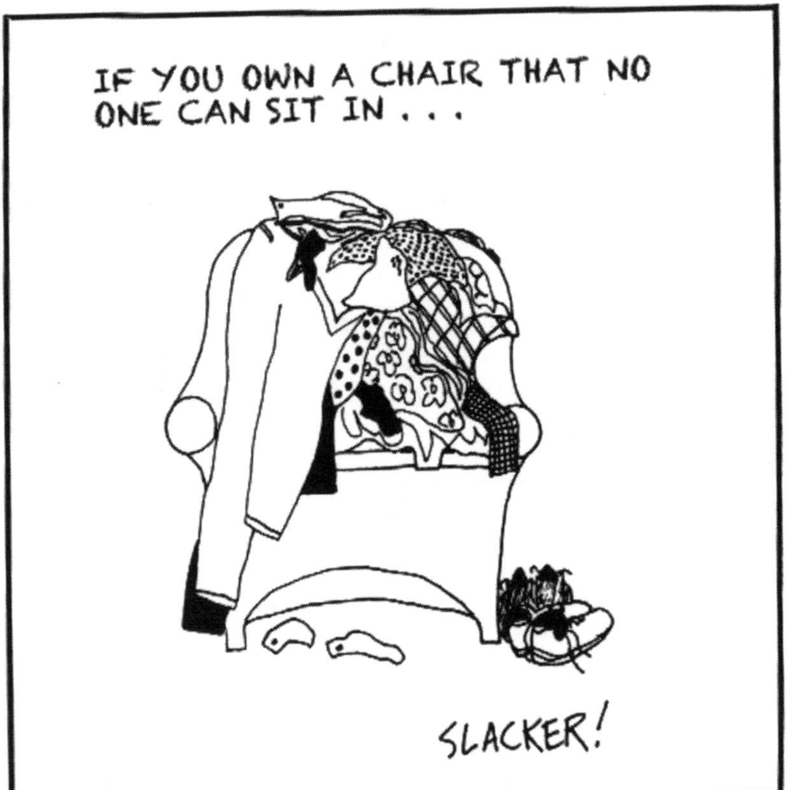
IF YOU OWN A CHAIR THAT NO ONE CAN SIT IN . . .
SLACKER!

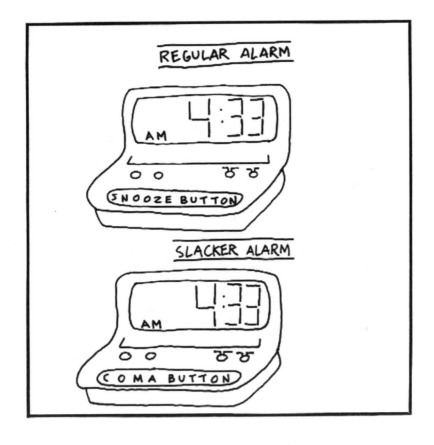

If you find yourself defined by four or more of the above characterizations, then you are likely headed for a life of financial ruin or stand-up comedy. In many cases, both. So, find something to do. I suggest anything. And do it every day. That's diligence. That's the opposite of being a slacker. That's work. That's what most of our parents did so we wouldn't have to . . . which is a bad idea. Don't leave your children money. Leave them a business where they have to work for money. Leave your children land or your home or your business, but don't leave them so much that they become rich slackers. The last check you write in your life should go to the undertaker, and that one should bounce. *Sorry, kids.*

Since I'm Protestant, I probably feel more inclined to say this, but it would be wise to recover the Protestant work ethic to stop the tide of slackers slacking. Somehow our Protestant work ethic has been removed, like a guy trying to smoke at a restaurant in California. I don't know what happened, but somehow there was a generation that neglected to pass it on to their children, so the next generation missed it by default. Some blame it on the baby boomers, whose parents indulged them. I am one of those children.

I've discovered that if you let your children complain their way out of things, they become lazy. In our love, we are unintentionally breeding a generation of slackers who have no concept that being Protestant means having a work ethic.

This is why the Bible makes fun of slackers.

Just listen to some of these barbs.

Proverbs 19:24 (ESV): "The sluggard buries his hand in the dish and will not even bring it back to his mouth." If you're fasting because you're too lazy to feed yourself—how lazy can you be? So lazy that you'd starve if you had to put your hand to your mouth I guess. This is not far from the truth. (Probably why it's in the Bible.) It seems that a lazy person's goal in life is to avoid movement, specifically the movement of bending over. Be honest. Even now when you drop something, do you give a grunt of annoyance because you have to bend over to pick it up? That's the type of slacking Solomon is writing about here.

Proverbs 22:13 (ESV): "The sluggard says, 'There is a lion outside! I shall be killed in the streets!'" Slackers are always making excuses about why they can't do something. It's not that they can't get up and go to work. It's that there's a lion outside. Possibly. You never know. Be safe. Stay in bed.

God's will is that we work diligently, and by pampering our children . . . well, I was going to write that we're losing our Protestant work ethic, but it's too late. It's lost. We have to regain it.

Let's start by stopping this talk of retirement.

What kind of message is that?

Retirement is not biblical. The Bible's idea of retirement is that we die. That's retirement. We don't work hard so we can stop working to wear yellow pants and saddle shoes with cleats. The mentality that we retire so we can play demonstrates just how lost our work ethic is. If we retire, it should be *to* something, not away from work. We retire so we can devote more time to ministry. We retire so we can start some new productive venture. But we don't just stop. That will not only kill us, but it's immoral. Retirement is the ultimate sin of omission.

Sorry, Gramps.

So, it's not only good to work, but it's God's will to work. That's why we do the best job that we can, because it's for Him. Because whatever kind of job we do will reflect on the One we follow, either positively or negatively. And He wants our work to reflect Him because we will influence someone by doing it.

Proverbs 22:29 (ESV): "Do you see a man skillful in his work? He will stand before kings; he will not stand before obscure men." The more excellent your work is (whatever it is, besides anything immoral), the more it will take you places you never thought possible. When I first started a career in stand-up comedy, an older, wiser comedian took me aside and asked me this question: "How much time do you spend working on your act each day?"

"What?"

I didn't understand the question.

This is comedy. It's not work, I thought.

Then he laid some enlightenment on me. He said, "Most comedians are so lazy they don't work on their acts at all. The comedians who do are the comedians who succeed. A really funny, naturally talented, but lazy comedian will eventually be passed up by a mildly funny guy who works really hard at it. He'll eventually become funnier than the more naturally talented guy, even if he only devotes two hours a day to his act."

Who knew?

Comedy is hard work.

That's true in whatever career you find yourself. Hard work pays off; not that two hours a day is hard work, but his example was relative. Two hours a day is hard work to a lazy person.

So, find something to do.

Then do it like you're doing it for God Almighty (because you are). This means showing up on time, not stealing things from work, doing the best job you can no matter what that job is, etc.

Do it diligently. (This means showing up daily.)

And finally, do it honestly.

Proverbs 20:10 (ESV): "Unequal weights . . . are an abomination to the Lord." This is probably one of the most neglected areas of the Christian life. Most often, we think of this as having to do with "not stealing stuff from work and being fair." That's part of it. The other part has to do with the quality of our work. If we don't give a job our all, then it's like stealing from our employer or our client or whoever we happen to work for. Giving a job just enough to get by. That's not honest. That's unequal weights.

And that's what happened to the Protestant work ethic—it lost its ethic. There's no morality to work anymore. People don't see the lack of effort they give their job as immoral. Welcome to the age of the Hedonistic Work Ethic, where children only mow the lawn when it's fun. We lost our work ethic because we no longer view "whoever we work for" as almighty God. When we stand before God we want Him to say, "Well done, good and faithful servant," not "Slacker be thy name."

Okay, break's over.

Back to work.

16

WITH A NEW AFTERWARD
(The Inspiring Success Story All because You Bought This Book)

....

Y ou have come a long way in my financial journey.
I hope it has inspired you not to be like me.

During our climb out of debt, some days I felt hopeful about the future, and some days I faced our bills: TWENTY different creditors, including hospital, dental, and credit card bills. Not to mention the $4.69 that I owed my mother-in-law for eating her bag of Doritos.

The fact that we're out of debt is absolutely amazing if you notice how dumb we were about money matters. (See the book you're reading now, mostly any page.) Amazing grace that saved a dunce like me. While I was writing this book, my editor kept asking me, "Do you think you'll be out of debt by the time the book is published?"

And I would always answer with an unequivocal "No."

Sure, I understood that it would make a tidy ending to a book about getting out of debt if the author actually got out of debt, but I couldn't promise that. The book was more about exposing our guts and not giving up while encouraging others to do the same. Letting people know that there'll be peaks and valleys and that someone else is going through the same thing.

Because finances can be so depressing, I didn't look at our bank account regularly. I knew our budget plan: spend less, pay down the debt. So, when I discovered that we owed half as much as I thought we did, I was ecstatic because that's the same day I discovered we could eliminate our debt.

This happy ending occurred the same day this manuscript was due.

Somebody at Moody Publishers has way more faith than I do.

I remember the day Dinika and I discovered we had enough cash to pay down our major credit cards. She told me what she wanted to do with the money, then I told her what I wanted to do with the money, and we experienced something new—a fight about having money. Suddenly, bank statements were fun to read.

We could eliminate all of our major credit cards. Hint: all our credit cards are major credit cards. It's not like we have a Dippin' Dots credit card. It's the ice cream of the future. So they'll scan the mark on your forehead. Watch out for that.

But it's true. We were able to reduce our debt significantly by paying everything off. One simple step that only took a year. It's a really long step. Then we burned the invoices while my wife and children prepared the s'mores. "Are you cold, children? Let me burn some more credit card applications."

We made it out of the hole in just over a year. Don't you love a good underdog story? Aren't you a Saints fan? (They're a football team.) I'm told Harry Potter is an underdog, but no one who has magical powers is an underdog. That's not even fair. But we all love underdog stories because most of us have been underdogs at some point in our lives. We can relate to the saga of the underdog: someone in unfavorable conditions struggling to overcome great odds. Sometimes we just have to overcome being odd first, which makes us even more of an underdog.

As an underdog in debt, that's what it's going to feel like. It's going to feel like a good disaster movie. It's like your luxury boat hit this huge boulder called debt and your world is sinking. You have to abandon ship. Now you're bouncing around the ocean, feeling cold and alone, waiting for the sharks to eat you (or loan officers). But you slowly begin the long swim to shore. That's the paying down of debt. It feels like you're not making progress, but you keep paddling your feet anyway. Then eighteen months later, you reach dry land. It's not easy, but once you reach dry land, you jump around and run to your spouse in slow motion on the beach. You probably wouldn't have been in this situation to begin with if you hadn't had a stupid boat. Who can afford boats these days? Sell the boat. Pay down your debt. Run toward her in slow motion someplace less expensive next time.

Maybe you're beginning this journey as an underdog, too. Good for you. Become your own underdog story. As an underdog, doggedly pursue a debt-free life. The important thing is that you have taken a step toward financial recovery by reading this book. (Or at least I have now that you bought my book. Thanks for that.) Don't worry, Underdog, you can do it. You can get out of debt and begin to build wealth and in fifteen years you can be a millionaire. If you happen to be alive in fifteen years, then no problem. But don't let death get you down . . . you're a Christian.

People will tell you it can't be done, but ignore my mother-in-law. If by reading this book all you do is get out of debt, then this is by far the best humor book you've ever read. I'd recommend it to many friends and relatives if I were you, especially if they're the same people who've been telling you for years that it's impossible to live debt free. I'm telling you it can be done. Dave Ramsey is telling you it can be done. I'm only telling you because Dave Ramsey told me. I've discovered that it takes many people telling you the same things repeatedly before you begin to believe them. Things like "Take my advice and dump him." Things like that. That's just the first sign of hope. After you believe them, you take action. Sometimes. Maybe you think about taking action for a few years and then a recession hits, your booking agency implodes, your wife's

401k vanishes, and then you find yourself without any money.

Boy, does your life stink.

Wait.

That's my life.

In any case, the point is, the end of this book could be the beginning of another for you. I hope this book has either encouraged you in your journey to financial recovery or inspired you to begin. If you've been afraid to delve into a financial planning book, fear no more. Go out and buy a copy of *Dave Ramsey's Total Money Makeover,* and you won't be sorry. (And no, I don't get a kickback for promoting his book.) I just happen to believe in his wisdom because Dave picked up his wisdom from someplace else, the Bible. Oddly enough, people don't realize the Bible is full of sound financial advice. Dave did, and he made a million telling people about it.

I just wanted to get out of debt and encourage others to do the same.

You will experience highs and lows as you pay off your bills, get out of debt, and begin to forge a new financial future as a new champion of capital instead of an underdog of debt. Or a king of cash instead of a chump of change. Or a gold medalist of gold instead of a dark horse of dinero. Or a . . . you get the idea—I own a thesaurus. (Just one of the advantages of having money.) It takes commitment, but if you keep at it, you'll begin to notice changes not only with your checkbook, but with you. Like, your nails get longer when you have money. Your spouse appears more attractive when you're not yelling at each other about the disconnected phone. Things like that.

They seem like small things, but the most important thing you can come away with is a heart that treasures different things. That's what will help you from repeating the same cycle. Dinika and I have been debt free before, but the effects were not lasting. That's why noticing the small changes becomes so encouraging. It lets you know that throughout this process God has been doing a work in your heart.

Before our money meltdown, I had enough frequent flyer miles for two first-class round-trip tickets to New York City, where I had planned to take my wife for a getaway weekend to take in a Broadway show, do some shopping, and fly home. Then our priorities changed. We never did take that trip. I eventually used those miles for work to save travel expenses to help pay down our debt. Sure, I'd like to do that trip someday, but I told myself, "Now is not the time. There's nothing good playing on Broadway."

Two other small examples.

While checking out my rental car this last weekend, the rental guy asked me if I'd like to upgrade to the next level of car for just five dollars a day. Before I started on this journey to a debt-free existence, I would have gone for the extra room. My family was meeting me in Grand Rapids, and we'd be on the road for two weeks. That was the reason I wanted to give myself for upgrading. *We need more space.* The real reason was that I didn't want to be seen driving a PT Cruiser. Have you seen this confused vehicle? It looks like it was in a time travel accident. But I gratefully declined his offer, keeping the PT Cruiser, which apparently only rental car agencies buy. (My apologies if you happen to own one. I'm sure you've learned from your mistake.) What does the PT stand for? Personal Tragedy . . . for buying it? Physical Training . . . from pushing it? Maybe it means Part-Time car.

Then I was at the Apple Store having my iPhone serviced by a genius when I noticed a nice new Hurley laptop backpack. My Incase backpack is frayed and split at the bottom, but it still holds the laptop. So far. The new backpack was eighty bucks, and I had just deposited seven checks from the last two weeks into the bank. I could afford it. I could pay cash. But I didn't. That's ninety more dollars for my Little Things List.

When we arrived home that next Sunday, Dinika handed our pastor's wife a check and said, "I'm giving this cheerfully. In case you can't tell. I'm very cheerful."

These are all good signs of heart transformation. Well, besides my wife gritting her teeth. Like all true spiritual growth, the radical shifts take time.

I am more like you than any financial guru you've ever read. I've gone from underdog to out-of-debt underdog. That should fill you with hope for the future. It hasn't been easy living out these practical little principles, but it has been worth it. Getting out of debt feels like a great accomplishment, but it's really only the first step. The next step is to never get into debt again.

That will tell us that it's all real.

Because I never want to be like myself again.

APPENDIX A
(or As I Like to Call It: Leftovers #1)

....

E ven a quick overview of what Jesus said about money is more revealing than the vast majority of books on personal finances (besides Dave Ramsey, who gets his wisdom from the Bible).

Here is list of things Jesus said about money:

Jesus said it before Bob Dylan, but you gotta serve somebody. It can be money or God, but it can't be both (Matthew 6:24). The drawback to worshiping money is that banks aren't open on Sundays, so you'll have to take time out of your workweek to worship. Besides, the Capital One praise band is lousy.

The focus of a house of worship should be prayer and kingdom things, not making change for a dollar (Matthew 21:12). Churches should take an offering, not offer a taking.

You should invest (Matthew 25:27). Heaven is like the New York Stock Exchange: You can't just waltz in without a mediator.

If God sends you somewhere to do something for Him, you won't need anything but God (Mark 6:8). And all the church planters said, "Get out!"

It's not how much you give, it's how much you *give* (Mark 12:41).

Money is the reason some people betray God (Mark 14:11). Awkward silence.

When you understand how great your debt is, you are tremendously thankful when it's forgiven (Luke 7:41–42). Banks are not forgiving.

Don't be anxious about life's necessities (Luke 12:22). The thing is, you should be so carefree and confident that God will give you everything you need, that you can sell your stuff and give to the poor. As God provides for you, you can provide for others. You can actually give your way out of debt (Luke 12:33). And all the church members said, "Get out!"

People who love money ridicule Christ (Luke 16:14). Show me a poor atheist, and I'll show you someone who won't say grace *or* pick up the check.

God holds us accountable for how we spend our money (Luke 19:15). Let the weight of that statement sink in. *God holds us accountable for how we spend our money.* That should change everything. We can either look at our bank statements now or later.

When there's a crisis, you need some cash. And a sword wouldn't hurt, either (Luke 22:36). Whenever I negotiate any type of loan, I always wear a sword. If the banker asks me about it, I just say, "I have penalties too."

People who hate giving to charity are thieves (John 12:5). I don't know what the stats on this are, because robbers don't keep good tax records.

Some people think they can buy God's favor with money (Acts 8:18). But that shouldn't keep you from writing a check.

People give sacrificially during times of revival (Acts 4:37). Oh, how we need revival.

Some people hang out with you only because they want your money (Acts 24:26). But I don't care. I like my wife.

Pastors shouldn't be known for loving money (1 Timothy 3:3). That's not enough to silence the prosperity preachers, though.

Loving money is linked to proud arrogant people, lovers of self, the unholy, and movie stars (2 Timothy 3:2). Not to be redundant.

You can be content with what you have because God will take care of you (Hebrews 13:5). And other slogans rejected by Wal-Mart.

APPENDIX B

How to Overcome Bitterness
(The Notes My Wife Found for Me
from Chapter 3)

....

Overcoming bitterness is something we all know how to do. We know it instinctively. Three simple steps. This is all part of taking responsibility for your role in the financial situation your family is in. Don't worry. At no point during this exercise will you be asked to close your eyes and imagine a bright future.

And the three steps are:

1. Lay your pride aside. (This is easier to do once you take a part-time job as a census worker.)

One day while discussing finances, my wife and I were at each other's throats (trying to determine who charged a tonsillectomy) when I paused and said, "Let's pray a moment." You'll find that prayer is often followed by apologies. Guys, this is where you have to initiate things, which is step 2.

2. Initiate reconciliation. (Sounds like there's a button to engage, but basically you just approach your spouse. Walk, don't run.)

3. Apologize and forgive.

If you're single, you can follow these steps by looking in the mirror. This will feel awkward, and it should. Who talks to themselves in the mirror? That's stupid. However, your financial woes are the fault of that person in the mirror. So, when creditors call, refer them to the person in the mirror. Good luck getting him or her to talk back. But now you have someone else to blame, and it's not that far from the truth.

If you want to recover financially, you and your spouse are going to have to do this together. If one of you isn't on board, it will not work. You both have to face your financial fears with each other. You both have to take responsibility, otherwise one of you will end up angry.

APPENDIX C

*A Bring-the-Conviction Moment about
Little Things Adding Up
(Chapter 7)*

....

Here's something to consider.

Jesus said that if we are faithful with a few things (or with little things), we will be faithful with more things. [32] So the question becomes, "How can we expect God to bless our efforts to get out of debt if we're not willing to sacrifice any of the little things that waste our money?" This becomes difficult to apply in a family, because everyone wants something different and everything that's wanted costs money. This is where, if you're the husband, leading your family spiritually comes in handy. Every day you have to model this attitude of being faithful in small things by making small sacrifices. It's a process that happens daily, slowly, and with some difficulty, just like spiritual growth. Every day we have to go back to the little things in both our financial and our spiritual lives, and trust that the little changes will add up to fruitful spiritual lives the same way that the little sacrifices we make to get out of debt will add up to a debt-free life.

APPENDIX D
Just Keep Repeating

....

STOP using credit cards.

Now.

Never. Ever. Never ever never ever.

Do me a favor right now. Pick one of your credit cards. That's right. Pick a card, any card. Look at how much you owe on that credit card. Now, name me all the swell stuff you bought. Right now. Don't hesitate, just rattle off all the fine, shiny stuff you bought. If you're like me, then you probably can't name most of what you bought. And saying, "$5,467.90 in food and beverages" doesn't count.

STOP using credit cards.

Now.

Never. Ever. Never ever never ever.

She's not that good a date.

APPENDIX E

Lemonade Stand Story
(Deleted from Chapter 5—Here for the First Time in Print)

....

Like many children, I built a lemonade stand. And like most cases, my dad was our only customer, but he bought one glass for five bucks. Still, it wasn't an encouraging business venture. The only thing it really taught me was "Don't worry, Dad will bail you out." This proved problematic once he died.

Our ten-year-old daughter, Eden, has been setting up a lemonade stand daily in our front yard. Our home is on a busy street, so she sets up a card table and sells Dixie cups filled with lemonade (already more cost-effective than the large glass I used as a kid) and necklaces that she and her business partners made. Yes, business partners. The little girl next door wrote up a contract. No joke. And my daughter's best friend, Cienna, gets a cut of the action, too, because she helped make the necklaces. Day after day, I am amazed at how much cash they rake in: $11 the first day, $22 the second day, $30 the day the park down the street had an event, and the list goes on. I thought about charging them

something for using our lawn, like a business lease. Every little bit helps
. . . to fund Starbucks.

They've even written a jingle to advertise. Choreographed, no less.
They all clap and sing, "Come and get the lemonade. Come and get the
jewelry. You know you're gonna love it. Cooooommmmmme and get it!"

Then one of them walks down the street with a sign that says, "Kids
jewelry 25 cents. Ice-cold lemonade 25 cents."

Cars pull over and order through their windows.

"Two glasses, please."

They don't know about the new Dixie cup changes to lemonade
stands, but they pay for them anyway. Some adults overpay, of course,
because all they know is that their dad once paid five bucks a glass, too.

Here's what I think is happening.

There is a residual of negative past lemonade stand experiences built
up that our children are reaping the rewards of. Every adult I've talked
to this about confesses to having a disappointing lemonade stand experience as a kid. Our experiences resulted in a collective silent vow. Every
adult with a bad lemonade stand experience has made a silent vow to
never let it happen to another child. In practical terms, whenever we
see a lemonade stand, we are bound by our unspoken oaths to buy a cup
and overpay for it. Our children are reaping the rewards of our failures
as lemonade stand entrepreneurs.

Her financial background is already better than mine. She's having
a positive money experience. Whereas I learned that Dad would bail
you out, my daughter is learning that if you are industrious, you can
make some money. Now she just needs to learn about price gouging.
Five bucks for a thimble of lemonade?

APPENDIX F
Money Lessons from Dad

....

Old habits die hard.

One of those old habits I owe to my dad, who always said, "You get what you pay for," which is every man's excuse for spending a lot of money on something. And we do it sincerely because our fathers taught us "you get what you pay for." What else did you expect to get? What you didn't pay for?

"Here's your garden hose."

"But I just put $300 down on a new car."

"$300 down? Hey, buddy, you get what you pay for, and at Mercedes that's a garden hose."

Whenever you pay for something, you get it, so you always get what you pay for. The thinking behind this phrase is that the more you pay for something, the better it is. That's what our dads are really trying to say, which turns out only to be true when it comes to hotel rooms.

One night in Chicago my flight was delayed until the next day. Being that airlines are more frugal with their cash than I am, they don't put you up for the night when the reason for the delay is snow. Stuck in Chicago and tired of traveling, I walked to the Hilton that's located in the airport and paid (charged) $250 for a room because "you get what you pay for." This was a nice room. I think. I was SLEEPING! As it turns out, you can also sleep for $49 a night at Day's Inn and also not notice the room. That's one thing being broke has cured me of, overspending for the sake of a five-dollar jar of peanuts in the minifridge. At least I think they were five dollars. I was SLEEPING.

APPENDIX G
Finis

....

You can stop reading now.
Hope you enjoyed it.

NOTES

....

1. Hebrews 4:13.

2. Matthew 6:21.

3. See appendix B.

4. He's on the $5,000 dollar bill.

5. Ecclesiastes 10:19.

6. Matthew 6:21.

7. Psalm 24:1.

8. Romans 8:32 (technically asked by God via the apostle Paul).

9. Proverbs 13:7.

10. www.pickpunch.com.

11. James Scurlock, *Maxed Out* (New York: Scribner, 2007), 48.

12. Jordan E. Goodman, *Master Your Debt* (Hoboken, NJ: Wiley, 2010), 1.

13. Dave Ramsey, *Total Money Makeover* (Nashville: Thomas Nelson, 2003, 2007), 23.

14. Psalm 42:5 ESV.

15. Michael Lewis, *The Big Short* (New York: Norton & Co., 2010).

16. Proverbs 17:16 ESV.

17. James Truslow Adams, *The Epic of America* (New York: Simon Publications, 2001).

18. John 10:10 ESV.

19. Romans 11:22 NKJV.

20. Stephen J. Nichols, *Jesus Made in America* (Chicago: InterVarsity Press, 2008), 19–98.

21. *Talladega Nights: The Ballad of Ricky Bobby*, Columbia Pictures, 2006.

22. David Platt, *Radical: Taking Back Your Faith from the American Dream* (Colorado Springs: Multnomah Books, 2010), Kindle location 239–42.

23. Proverbs 13:7.

24. Ecclesiastes 9:11 ESV.

25. 1 Timothy 6:17 ESV.

26. 3 John 1:2 NKJV.

27. Luke 6:38.

28. Leviticus 23.

29. You can read the story of Zacchaeus in the gospel of Luke, chapter 19.

30. Romans 8:32.

31. Proverbs 13:11 ESV.

32. Luke 16:10.

ACKNOWLEDGMENTS

....

This book would have been impossible without my wife, Dinika, of course, who could have killed the whole project simply by refusing to use cash. As always, but probably not mentioned enough, aloud, in front of dinner guests, I am grateful for her support in all creative endeavors.

For the second time in a row, the skillful mechanics of Marshall Allen's insightful editorial eye fixed this thing up good. Keen in his double role as literary agent, he gives me such scrupulous attention that he often makes me feel like I'm his only client. It is a privilege to work with not only a talented man, but a godly one.

If I have not mentioned Dave Ramsey (no relation) enough, then I must do so one last time, because if not for Dave Ramsey, I would be thanking Suze Orman. Seriously, thanks for the two free books, Dave. The proof is in the pudding, which is a horrible place to look for anything.

Thanks to everyone at Emmaus Church in Redlands, California, for being so understanding and not judging us in the least for all our financial shortcomings. I hope. This will be the first time some of you hear about all this.

Finally, I want to thank Madison Trammel and everyone at Moody Publishers who is hoping that the second time's a charm.

So, Christopher, do you think this would make a good screenplay?

YOUR MONEY MAP

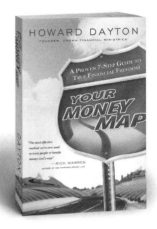

By revealing key biblical principles of finance, *Your Money Map* steers readers toward the clear biblical basics of money management through seven financial destinations that anyone can reach. No matter how distant the end goals may seem, *Your Money Map* provides realistic steps and all the necessary tools to achieve them. The end result? True freedom to invest your time and resources in furthering The Great Commission.

978-0-8024-6868-0   Also available as an EBook 978-1-57567-314-1

FREE AND CLEAR

Becoming debt-free may seem an impossible dream for many, but it is actually an attainable goal according to Howard Dayton. He overcame his own struggle with debt by applying God's principles to managing his finances, principles he lays out in this practical, encouraging, never-give-up book.

978-0-8024-2257-6   Also available as an EBook 978-1-57567-461-2

MOODY
PUBLISHERS

moodypublishers.com

MASTER YOUR MONEY

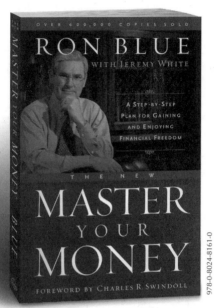

OVER 600,000 COPIES SOLD

RON BLUE
WITH JEREMY WHITE

A STEP-BY-STEP
PLAN FOR GAINING
AND ENJOYING
FINANCIAL FREEDOM

THE NEW

MASTER
YOUR
MONEY

FOREWORD BY CHARLES R. SWINDOLL

978-0-8024-8161-0

Also available as an EBook 978-1-57567-537-4

Finally … a financial planning book that presents concepts in an easy-to-understand format. Ron Blue extracts principles from God's Word and applies them to your financial portfolio. Ron's professional experience in financial planning will be an asset to you and to your family for generations to come. This second edition includes important updates and new content you won't want to miss.

MOODY
PUBLISHERS

moodypublishers.com